WILLIAM RANDOLPH
HEARST
and the American Century

WILLIAM RANDOLPH HEARST
and the American Century

Nancy Whitelaw

620 South Elm Street, Suite 223
Greensboro, North Carolina   27406
http://www.morganreynolds.com

WILLIAM RANDOLPH HEARST AND THE AMERICAN CENTURY

Library of Congress Cataloging-in-Publication Data

Whitelaw, Nancy.
    William Randolph Hearst and the American century / Nancy Whitelaw.—
Rev. ed.
      p. cm. — (Makers of the media)
    Includes bibliographical references and index.
    ISBN 1-931798-35-4 (lib. bdg.)
      1. Hearst, William Randolph, 1863-1951—Juvenile literature. 2. Publishers and publishing—United States—Biography—Juvenile literature. 3. Newspaper publishing—United States—History—19th century—Juvenile literature. 4. Newspaper publishing—United States—History—20th century—Juvenile literature. [1. Hearst, William Randolph, 1863-1951. 2. Publishers and publishing.]
I. Title. II.
Series.
    Z473.H4W48 2004
    070.5'092—dc22

2003024612

Dedicated to Patty Baerwald—with love and thanks for introducing me to Conflict Dispute Resolution

Contents

William Randolph Hearst

Chapter One

Willie

William Randolph Hearst had many reasons for wanting to own a newspaper, and what they all had in common was his desire for power. He wanted to expose lying politicians; to help readers understand their city, state, country, and world; and to influence public opinion with editorials. He wanted to become mayor of New York City, governor of New York State, and then president of the United States. He also wanted to make lots of money.

William Hearst's ambitions were ingrained early, especially since his mother was convinced he could do no wrong. A mischievous boy, when Willie was four years old, he used a hose to squirt his dancing teacher, soaking the man's black silk knee breeches, silk stockings, and dancing pumps. Then he led a group of his friends to the dance school and encouraged them to throw stones at the building—all in response to a well-deserved scolding.

One day he played with his mechanical mouse while his mother was serving tea in the living room. He waited until the ladies sat down, balancing cups, saucers, and plates on their laps. Then he aimed the mouse into the middle of the group and let it go.

Another day he took half a dozen pie plates from the kitchen. He lined them in a row on his bedroom floor, putting a flare in the middle of each one. After everyone had gone to sleep that night, he lit the flares and ran out into the hall yelling, "Fire!" He ran back into his room, locked his door from the inside, and waited. He didn't wait long. The panicked adults who came running saw a red glare under Willie's door and they smelled smoke. One called the fire department while others battered down the door. When they reached Willie, he told them gleefully that they had fallen for his April Fool's joke.

Sometimes his mother laughed with him about his pranks. Sometimes she said she wished he would stop playing tricks. Always she told him that he was forgiven. She would give anything to her son—a pony and cart, a Punch and Judy puppet show, all the money he could spend.

Phoebe Hearst, Willie's mother, adored her only child. She loved to have him close to her. No matter what he did, she said, "Bless his little heart, he is a very good boy." She added, "I scarcely ever leave Willie with anyone now. He is a real little calf about me." She taught Willie to read when he was four years old.

George Hearst, Willie's father, adored his son too.

Young William Randolph Hearst was fond of pranks and practical jokes.

But he didn't see much of him because his silver mines kept him busy away from home. When George did come home, he didn't want to spend his precious family time disciplining his son.

Willie's father and mother had many differences. George was twenty-two years older than Phoebe. He was over six feet tall; she was five feet tall. He disliked fancy clothes; she was known for her exquisite wardrobe. He was more often at work than at home; she loved decorating her home and entertaining in it. He was friendly and outgoing; she was reserved and shy. He was fascinated with politics; she was fascinated with culture and the arts. He paid no attention to his son's education. He said that reading, writing, and spelling were unimportant: "If b-u-r-d doesn't spell bird, what in hell does it spell?" Phoebe was a former teacher.

Willie was born in an exciting time and place. Gold and silver fever struck California in the mid-1800s. Pioneers came from all over the country to seek their fortune in this frontier with beautiful scenery, a gentle climate, and the promise of riches. In San Francisco, Willie loved to go down to the docks to see the sailing ships, the cargo ships, and the steamers as they entered and left the Pacific Ocean harbor.

In 1873, Willie's mother decided that her son needed to broaden his horizons. They planned an eighteen-month trip to Europe that would include both sightseeing and education. His mother said: "We will study all the time we are gone and improve all we can." To make sure of this, they brought along a Harvard tutor

Willie's mother, Phoebe Hearst, was devoted to her only son.

for Willie. It was to be his first trip abroad and he was excited about the trip.

Perhaps Willie had never seen poverty before. In Ireland, he was overwhelmed by the poor living conditions. His mother said, "he wanted to give away all his money and clothes." In other places, he saw the life his mother wanted him to become accustomed to living. In England, he decided that he would like to live in a home like Windsor Castle. One of their favorite pastimes was visiting castles and mansions, dreaming about having the same elegance back in the States. His mother bought linens, silver, and stemware in preparation for furnishing the castle of her dreams in America. In France, Willie asked his mother if she would buy the Louvre museum for him. He toured art galleries in Great Britain and on the continent, and collected stamps, coins, and decorated beer steins. He learned a little German and some French. In Rome, he and his mother received a papal blessing and toured the art and history exhibits.

Most people who met him thought Willie was shy. Although he was often quiet, he was ambitious. Once he was shown a historical treasure, a light that had not been extinguished for a thousand years. "I'd like to put out that light," said Willie. "Isn't there some way it can be done?" Even then, Willie wanted to make his mark on the world.

When they returned to America, they found that George Hearst had lost a lot of money in his investments and businesses. Phoebe asked immediately how they would pay for a private school for Willie. He should

George Hearst, Sr. owned several California gold mines and aspired to hold a political office.

go to private school, she said, so that he would make friends whose parents were socially prominent. No, said George, he should go to a public school so that he would meet ordinary people. Lack of money was the deciding factor. Willie went to public school.

No one is sure why Willie went to four different schools between 1874 and 1878. Maybe Willie's behavior forced the transfers. Maybe his mother decided that none of the schools was good enough for her son. In any case, he continued to enjoy life and to take pleasure in surprising people. He bragged to his father in a letter: "Bunny [Willie's rabbit] took some champagne last night and it made him tight; Mama was very much provoked with me but mad as she was she could not help laughing at him."

In 1879, Willie and his mother went to Europe again, this time with a friend instead of a tutor. Willie's friend was more fun than the tutor. He and Willie used bent pins to catch goldfish in a public fountain. When they were ordered to stay in the apartment for punishment, they amused themselves by tying a string to a cat's tail. The crazed animal destroyed curtains and furniture and smashed right through a china cabinet. Again, the boys were ordered to stay in the apartment. Willie had a small cannon, so he amused himself by shooting at pigeons outside the window.

In another hotel, Willie and his friend had a toy gun with a blank cartridge that shot with considerable power. Willie rested the butt of the gun on the floor and drove the ramrod into the barrel. Bam! The ramrod rose with force and stuck into the plaster ceiling. A maintenance man came to repair the damage. While he was working, the whole ceiling came down on him.

After they returned to America, Willie discovered a new source of entertainment. He found romance, color, and action in the glorious California Theater in San Francisco, both in the beauty of the building itself and in the comedies, tragedies, and musicals that were performed there. Willie announced that he wanted to be an actor. Never mind that he was shy. Never mind that his mother believed that stage people were common and vulgar. He liked the spectacle, the fantasy, and the drama of shows.

Soon, George's financial situation improved. Ever ready to take risks, he bought thousands of acres of land in California, Texas, Arizona, and New Mexico, as well as in Mexico. He reasoned that some of the land would be valuable for mining, some for grazing, and some for future developments.

In the fall of 1879, sixteen-year-old Willie was sent to St. Paul's School, a private college-preparatory school in New Hampshire. Almost immediately, he was homesick for his mother, unhappy with the required Episcopal church services, dissatisfied with the food, and bored by the classes that included Church and Sacred History. But his grades were average, and he seemed to have calmed down. His family received no bad reports about his behavior.

Her son was doing well, but Phoebe was not. She worried constantly about him, and she missed him terribly. She suffered from generally poor health anyway, and Willie's absence made her suffer more. Gradually, she became involved with writers and artists, and delved into charity work. She discovered and funded young people who showed promise but lacked money. With her generous help, the first Hearst Free Kindergarten opened in an area where many poor immigrants lived.

In 1880, George bought the *San Francisco Examiner*. Both he and seventeen-year-old Willie were pleased with the purchase. George wanted to use the newspaper to make himself known as a potential candidate for political office, but since Willie had given up his dream of acting, he wanted a career in the newspaper business after he graduated from college.

Phoebe did not like the idea of journalists in the family and was delighted when Willie passed the tests for admission to Harvard. After less than two years at St. Paul's School, Phoebe took her son to Cambridge, Massachusetts, to help him settle at the college. She stayed with him for several days to decorate his room in Matthews Hall and to stock a fine library for him.

By age nineteen, Willie was tall and slender. He had three distinguishing characteristics—his voice, his eyes, and his clothes. He thought his voice was embarrassingly high and girlish. His blue-gray eyes showed exceptionally large, white irises that made it seem as if he were staring. His favorite clothes were made from bright plaids, and he wore loud neckties.

The move to Harvard was almost more than Willie could stand. In San Francisco he was doted on, and his

Willie was expelled from Harvard because of poor grades and bad behavior.

every wish was granted. At Harvard, his time and actions were regimented, much more so than at St. Paul's School, and he was not special to anyone there. He was shy about meeting people and making friends. After just a few weeks, he wrote to his mother, "I am beginning to get awfully tired of this place, and I long to go out west somewhere where I can stretch myself without coming in contact with the narrow walls."

Gradually, he began to accept his new life, especially his new social life. Because he learned quickly, he didn't spend much time studying. He befriended a group of young men who also paid little attention to classes. They enjoyed theater trips to Boston and beer parties. He became known around campus as Champagne Charlie's master. Champagne Charlie was his pet: an alligator that sometimes went visiting with him. Willie fed Champagne Charlie liquor at parties.

Willie spent generously, and his friends relied on him to help with cash. It was no wonder that he wrote to his mother: "My financial condition is the same as usual. I am busted." He admitted that he had a spending problem and told her he might work on it: "I think I shall take a Political Economy course in hopes that it will teach me to regulate my money affairs better."

Champagne Charlie was not Willie's only amusement. He found plenty of extracurricular activities to occupy himself with. Once, Willie and his friends threw oranges at policemen after a long night out in local taverns. He threw custard pies at performers in a theater. Apparently, he worried a little about his behavior.

He wrote his parents that he had gotten into trouble at school, but he did not elaborate. He signed the letter, "your reformed child."

In his first year at Harvard, Willie signed up for—and then dropped—Latin, Greek, and philosophy. He changed his major from philosophy to English. He became active in the failing college newspaper, the *Lampoon*. Using some of the energy that he didn't spend on his courses, he sold advertisements to local shopkeepers, created a program to ask for funds from Harvard students and graduates, and worked to increase circulation. Soon the *Lampoon* budget was in the black. Willie suddenly saw himself as a success, and he looked to the future with a grand dream. He sent a *Lampoon* financial report to his mother, writing, "Show this to Papa, and tell him just to wait till Gene [a college chum] and I get hold of the old *Examiner* and run her in the same way."

Willie studied the *San Francisco Examiner* with new fascination, believing that he could manage it better than his father did. In fact, he believed he could run any of his father's businesses—mining, ranching, investments—as well as the paper. He asked his father to consider him as a potential associate: "Will you kindly take some slight notice of your only son?"

Willie appeared shy and quiet much of the time. But occasionally he put on a show that brought him instant attention. A rumor circulated that he once brought a donkey into an empty classroom, knowing that the professor would soon appear. He put a sign around the

animal's neck which read, "Now there are two of you."
When his favored candidate, Democrat Grover Cleveland, won the presidential race in 1884, Willie threw a huge party with a lot of beer, fireworks, a brass band, and general rowdiness. The party continued until the police broke it up.

In September, Willie had to tell his parents that Harvard would accept him back only conditionally. He had to improve his grades and exhibit appropriate behavior at all times. Phoebe rushed to Cambridge to see how she could help her son. She found that Willie was drinking too much, partying too often, and generally showing an immaturity that left her weeping with frustration. But she proposed a plan. On her part, she would hire a tutor for her son. On his part, he would promise to try harder.

Despite her efforts, Willie didn't try harder. Instead, he continued to enjoy an active social life at dinners, theaters, and parties. He also continued to spend extravagantly, both on himself and on his friends. Despite Phoebe's pleas, he was suspended from Harvard.

Willie had grown tired of college anyway. He was like his father, he decided. George had never been interested in education, either. They were alike in another way too: both were interested in politics. A couple of years earlier, George had run for governor of California on the Democratic ticket. He had lost, but wanted to run again. Willie had dreams of running for office, and in his dreams, he always won. Sure that he could make his mark on the country, he moved to Washington

D.C. Phoebe believed that Willie could do anything he really wanted to, so she bought him a home in Washington to help him establish a career.

Now that he was free from college restrictions, Willie felt more confident. He wrote to his father, telling him how to make the *Examiner* a better paper. "If you should make over to me the *Examiner*—with enough money to carry out my schemes, I'll tell you what I would do!" His suggestions included: hire better reporters; write articles like those in the *New York World*; stop printing colorless writing; divide the paper into seven, instead of nine, columns; and advertise more widely. He ended his letter "Well, good-by. I have given up all hope of having you write to me."

Willie had three interests in Washington: Congress; American history; and tall, slender, blue-eyed Eleanor Calhoun, an actress. Phoebe was aghast at the idea of an actress in the family. She offered to pay for Eleanor's study of drama if the actress would move to Europe. Eleanor accepted. She was out of Willie's mind as soon as she was out of his sight.

In September 1885, Harvard accepted Willie again on the same conditions as before—improved grades, appropriate behavior. He didn't have time to improve his grades before he failed the appropriate behavior condition. He sent chamber pots to his professors with their names engraved on the bottoms, and was expelled.

His mother wept. His father took the expulsion calmly, until Willie told him, "I want the *San Francisco Examiner.*" George wanted his son to be more than the owner of a newspaper, especially owner of a failing newspaper. He offered to let him supervise one of his cattle ranches in Mexico. Willie refused. George offered him supervision of an American ranch. Willie refused again. He offered to make him manager of a mine. "It's a wonderful mine," answered Willie, "and you are very kind, but I'd rather have the *Examiner*."

When his father rejected him again, Willie moved to New York and became a reporter for the *New York World*, published by Joseph Pulitzer. Although he was blind and plagued with severe nervous disorders, Pulitzer had remained on top of the competition in New York for years. Willie was determined to join him.

Chapter Two

Newspaperman

After only a few months in New York, Willie was summoned home when his father won a six-year term in the U.S. Senate. The *Examiner*, he was told, was his.

Willie, now sometimes called W. R., had grand dreams for his paper. Now twenty-four, he wrote to his father, "One year from the day I take hold of the thing our circulation will have increased ten thousand." One week after the first issue came out under his name, he called the *Examiner*, "The Largest, Brightest and Best Newspaper on the Pacific Coast." The truth was the paper had a circulation of less than 23,000 and an office with just two telephones, one printing press, and an "art department" that consisted of two men working an old chalk process over a coal and oil stove.

The new publisher became known around town for his handsome blond looks, his gaudy ties, and his collection of fascinating walking sticks, including one that whistled. Around other newspapermen, however, the gossip was different. Fremont Older, a reporter at another paper, said that newspaper writers knew "this young Harvard man was not to be taken seriously. Of course he was nothing more than the son of a millionaire who thought it would be good fun to 'take a fling' at journalism."

Older was partly right, but W. R. had picked up many ideas and insights while working at Joseph Pulitzer's newspaper. He offered handsome salaries to the most colorful and dramatic writers he could find and quickly fired any writer who wrote what he considered to be a dull article.

W.R. was also polticically active. He supported reforms in government. He organized a drive to defeat a city charter that he said would hurt the poor. He led a campaign against the growing political power of railroads. For these reform movements, Hearst gained respect among both general readers and politicians, though the audience he cared about most was the general public. He told his reporters, "We don't want fine writing in a newspaper. Don't write a single line he [a blue-collar worker] can't understand and wouldn't read."

To gain support for the *Examiner*, W. R. gave spectacular picnics and parties for influential people. He rode from city to city on a train advertising his paper, hosting meals, and throwing flowers along the way. He even reduced advertising rates to bring in more ads. He published popular songs and created a column dedicated to the working man. He printed at least one sensational story on every front page.

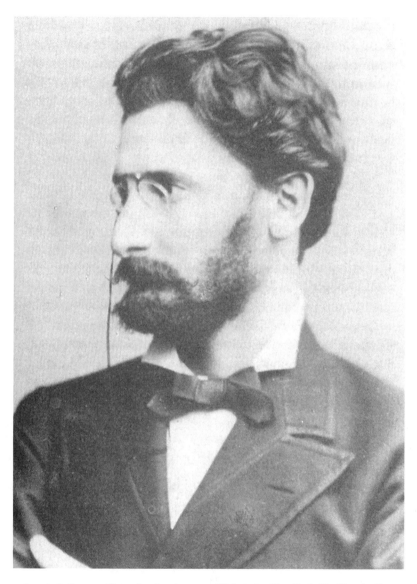

Joseph Pulitzer, a Hungarian immigrant, published the *New York World*, a leading newspaper of the day.

Like editors at the *New York World*, Hearst encouraged reporters to invent drama behind otherwise common news events like murders and scandals. He freely admitted his use of sensational stories: "I had to get the people to look at the paper." When Sarah Bernhardt, an internationally famous actress, appeared in an opium den in Chinatown, W. R. made a big story of it. Another time, one of his female reporters pretended that she was destitute, let herself be taken to the city hospital, and wrote an exposé of the horrible conditions there. He hired a sportsman to bring a grizzly bear from the mountains of southern California to present to the Golden Gate Park. He sent an engaged couple and their minister up in a balloon called the "Examiner" to be married in the air. He asked his father to exert pressure on his fellow legislators to support the paper and to encourage their constituents to buy it. He boasted that the *Examiner* had "the most elaborate local news, the freshest social news, the latest and most original sensations." Eventually, he enlarged the paper to eight pages.

To his mother, he complained: "I don't suppose that I shall live more than three or four years if this strain keeps up." He admitted, "The newspaper business is no fun and I had no idea quite how hard a job I was undertaking." His messages to his father, however, were different. He bragged: "I will constitute a revolution in the sleepy journalism of the Pacific slope and will focus the eyes of all that section on the *Examiner*."

Four months after W. R. took over the paper, both circulation and advertising income were on the rise but it was still losing money. W. R.'s showmanship and determination brought circulation to nearly 40,000, but still the paper lost money. Hearst, Sr. paid out $300,000 in one year to meet the paper's expenses. W. R. did not trouble himself with financial matters; he continued to pay top dollar for reporters and editors and to stage elaborate parties.

In one year, W. R. spent more than Phoebe and George spent together, even though Phoebe traveled luxuriously and George kept racehorses. A financial adviser suggested that W. R. live on a fixed allowance. He would draw no more than $5,000 a month from his parents until 1888, at which time, he promised the *Examiner* would stand on its own. His parents approved the plan, but despite their agreement, W. R. continued to spend freely on the newspaper. He also bought his own steam yacht for commuting across San Francisco Bay. And he lavished money on his mistress Tessie Powers, a waitress whom he had met while at Harvard. His mother criticized the affair that society frowned on, but W. R. made no attempt to hide his relationship.

By 1899, George Hearst had given over $750,000 to the *Examiner*. He saw no chance of a profit as long as W. R. kept hiring workers at enormous salaries and spending lavishly on what he thought were crazy stunts to improve circulation. And like her son, Phoebe was spending money on a grander scale than ever. She insisted that the family buy a handsome house in a high-society section of Washington. Then she traveled to Europe and Russia to study educational systems. George reviewed his finances and told his son he would receive no more family money.

W. R. complained that George had just spent $40,000 on a racehorse. How could he justify this expenditure while refusing his son the small allowance of $5,000 a month? He told George to cut down on his own expenses, beginning with selling his stable of racehorses. He said that the *Examiner* was on the verge of a big breakthrough in finances. If George would just send him $50,000, he could build a new newspaper plant, and perhaps he would buy a New York newspaper. Satisfied that his father would send him the requested money, W. R. went to Europe to buy a large number of art pieces and antiques, feeling sure that his every purchase would be a fine investment as well as a joy to own.

W. R. went to Europe on his shopping trip, but neither his father nor his mother offered the expected money. Nonetheless, W. R. figured out a way to get the money he wanted. He went to a Democratic chairman, a friend of the family, and told him that he knew he could turn a profit if only he had a little more investment money from his father. The chairman asked George Hearst for a $100,000 contribution to the party, and George signed a check immediately. The chairman turned over half the contribution to W. R., justifying the expenditure as a contribution to an active supporter of the party.

When George died of cancer in February 1891, he left his estate of about $20,000,000 to his wife. He left nothing to his twenty-seven-year-old son. Being left out of the will dismayed W. R. for two reasons: he needed money, and he felt humiliated by his father's lack of respect for him. He couldn't get Phoebe to sympathize. She knew all about his reckless spending, and besides, she was distressed by his relationship with Tessie Powers. Still, she couldn't resist giving him money for a trip abroad, even though she must have known that she was paying for Tessie's trip as well.

While W. R. was in Egypt, he did a little newspaper business. He wanted some photographs of the tombs of Egyptian kings that had never before been taken. These photographs would be a scoop for the *Examiner*. Hearst set up flashlights for illumination and shot the photos. Besides the pictures, he brought back a collection of mummies and some new sculptures.

He made plans to live on his father's ranch near Pleasanton. George had built the home so he could live near the racetrack. W. R. paid no attention to the fact that this was now his mother's house. He called in an architect to discuss modernizing it, enlarging it, and creating exhibit rooms for his growing collection of artifacts. When his mother discovered what he was doing, she said, "He is going too far." She felt that W. R.'s appropriation of the ranch, his affair with Tessie, and his general attitude toward work and money were leading him to destruction. She arrived in San Francisco late in 1893. No one knows what happened next. Maybe she spoke to Tessie herself; maybe she sent someone to speak for her. In any case, Tessie disappeared, leaving W. R. despondent.

Although depressed, W. R. continued to throw himself into the *Examiner*. He did not pretend to dig deeply into news stories; his was not an intellectual newspaper. W. R. relied instead on extravagant headlines, simple language and concepts, and lots of illustrations. A journalist wrote later, "The *Examiner* was a madhouse inhabited by talented and erratic young men. They had a mad boss, one who flung away money and cheered them on as they made newspaper history."

W. R. saw one of his dreams fulfilled—the *Examiner* finally made a profit. Hearst, whom many had begun calling the Chief, worked well with most of his employees, was always courteous, and complimented them when appropriate. He even did some of the writing himself: "I am probably one of those who write worse, and still I can express my own thoughts better than anyone else can express them for me."

Hearst didn't waver in his taste for sensationalism or his zeal for reform. He continued to believe that he could change the system that oppressed the middle and lower classes. He supported union labor and an eight-hour workday. He pushed for popular election of U.S. senators (who were then elected by state legislatures). He insisted that the Southern Pacific Railroad pay the $27 million debt it owed to the federal government. He wrote about corruption in the city system. He published "Hospital Horrors," a series of articles describing deplorable conditions at city and county hospitals. Defying the tradition that women belonged in the home, he invited women to publish an issue of the *Examiner*. All the advertising proceeds from that issue went to charities chosen by women. Opinions on the women's issue differed. Some men poked fun at the women, accusing them of playing at business. But many women and some men accepted the achievement as proof that women could succeed.

Hearst believed it was time to modernize. He bought land and asked his architect to create the most modern newspaper plant in the country. The new building included a mezzanine where spectators could watch the linotype operator set type and the proofreaders at work. They could see the photo engraver develop negatives and then create a design in relief that could be printed. They saw the pages pressed under a roller, baked on a steam table, and then poured into a box and doused with hot metal. Then they saw that product go through the presses and into the delivery room.

Sometime in 1894, Tessie returned and W. R. welcomed her back into his life. This time he was more discreet about the relationship, afraid that his mother's displeasure might mean an end to the money she supplied him. He tried to make a financial bargain with his mother, asking her for a guaranteed monthly allowance of $2,500. In return, he promised not to ask for an extra thousand here and there. Phoebe refused.

Tessie soon became seriously ill, both mentally and physically. W. R. sent her to a convalescent home in upstate New York.

Chapter Three

Newspaper War

While he enjoyed the *Examiner*, Hearst wanted a newspaper in New York City. He saw potential readers everywhere in this city bustling with elevated trains, delivery wagons, gentlemen with grand mustaches, ladies with long skirts, horseless carriages, and thousands of immigrants. He bid unsuccessfully for two New York papers, the *Herald* and the *Sun*. Then he bid for the *Journal*, a paper known as a scandal sheet, with a declining circulation of 77,000. The owner offered to sell Hearst half interest for $180,000. Hearst replied that he would not buy less than whole interest, and that he would not pay more than $180,000. The owner gave in, and Hearst got the paper on his terms.

Hearst's dream for his new paper was to beat his old employer, Joseph Pulitzer and the *New York World*, in every kind of competition—circulation, advertising, and profits. His first move was to lower the price of the *Journal* to a penny, one cent less than that of the *World*.

In just a few months, circulation of the *Journal* was over 100,000. Hearst made improvements in production and editorial processes: new techniques in setting type, more effective printing process, halftone photographs, a complete section of colored comics, mass-production of the pages, bold headlines, and the latest in mechanical aids.

He planned to hire away Pulitzer's best reporters by offering them larger salaries. Hearst offered the money, and several *World* writers accepted. As soon as he discovered the ploy, Joseph Pulitzer offered his former staff members more money than W. R. did. They returned to the *World*. Twenty-four hours after their return to Pulitzer, they accepted Hearst's offer of even higher wages.

Pulitzer dropped that struggle there, but the competition continued. Pulitzer hired a band for publicity. Hearst hired five bands. Pulitzer sent two reporters to South Africa. Hearst sent reporters to London, Cuba, the Balkans, Alaska, and Venezuela. Hearst sent coffee and sandwich wagons around to the poor, and even gave away sweaters when the weather was particularly cold. Pulitzer held out the hope that Hearst would "bankrupt his mother, go broke, and return to California."

The two papers had a lot in common. They used a simple, straightforward style to get their readers' attention and support. They both appealed to the masses by urging reform that would benefit everyday people. Both publishers believed sincerely that the underdog should be defended. They published stories about the homeless, and about poor people they believed were wrongfully accused of crimes. Both men were concerned about the plight of the thousands of immigrants who arrived in this country without either English language or job skills, and both supported increasing the number of soup kitchens for the poor. They also discussed cultural changes, including the growing "woman question." They wrote about women who smoked in public, and even pictured women wearing the latest style—bloomers.

Another element both papers had in common was their inclusion of comics, still a fairly new innovation in journalism. Each of the papers hired a cartoonist who created a comic series about a child who wore a yellow dress and was called the Yellow Kid. The two papers became known as the Yellow Papers, and gradually, their style of sensational writing became known as "yellow journalism."

W. R. made the most of the new term "yellow journalism" by turning it into an advertisement. He hired a group of bicycle riders, dressed them in yellow, and sent them from San Francisco to New York. These riders carried letters from postmasters in San Francisco to postmasters all along the route. The content of the letters was unimportant; the importance lay in the publicity given to these Yellow Fellows by the *Journal*.

Hearst knew that the public was more attracted to entertainment than to information. He used sensationalism to lure readers into an informative story. When human body parts were found floating in the East River, Hearst reporters wrote about the discovery with drama

Hearst used billboards to advertise the *Journal* and to announce his political views.

and suspense. First, they wrote about investigators finding an arm. Then, a leg. Then, another leg. The reporters created a tale of mystery and intrigue. To top it all off, they investigated the case thoroughly and beat the New York Police Department in finding a solution to the murder.

At other times, Hearst spent thousands of dollars sending correspondents to explore and report on important activities all over the world—the Greco-Turkish war, the sixtieth anniversary of Queen Victoria's coronation, and the Klondike gold rush in Alaska.

In a move to win subscribers from the *Journal*, Pulitzer lowered the price of the *World* to one penny. The good news for the *World* was that this move brought them 80,000 more subscribers, probably many of them former *Journal* subscribers. The bad news was that the *World* lost a lot of advertisers because it had to increase advertising rates to make up for the lower price per issue. Some of these advertisers moved to the *Journal*, where W. R. did not raise his rates. At the same time, Hearst lured Pulitzer's business manager to the *Journal*. Still Pulitzer refused to worry. He said, "He [Hearst] can't last. Even the Hearst fortune and the *San Francisco Examiner* can't keep him going much longer."

W. R. became involved in politics, and was eager to influence the 1896 presidential election. With his usual exuberance, he supported Democrat William Jennings Bryan, a silver-tongued orator with strong views about the economy. Another publisher might have cut down on his editorial opinions when he lost both readers and advertisers because of his political stance. But Hearst increased his support of Bryan and even created a fund-raising program for him. He declared that the *Journal* would match every dollar donation to the Bryan campaign with a dollar of its own. The paper lost money on this scheme, and Bryan lost the election to Republican William McKinley.

Hearst supported another unpopular cause: the right of women to vote. He said, "You cannot take a woman's son, and send him to war to be shot, unless you give her the right to vote about that war." He hired Susan B. Anthony, a famous advocate of women's suffrage, to write a column for the *Examiner*.

He was involved in local politics as well. W. R. wrote strong articles and editorials about New York City leaders who tried to use their power to influence the sale of a profitable gas franchise. He kept up a constant fight against the growing monopoly of the Southern Pacific Railroad. The railroad retaliated by falsely accusing him of taking bribes. Even though Hearst was cleared, his reputation suffered.

Politically, W. R. was eager to broadcast his views. Personally, he was very different. One of his editors said that his boss had two distinct personalities. As a newspaperman he was brazen. As a public person, he was shy to the point of lowering his eyes and not carrying on a conversation. One business associate said of him: "He is genuinely shy with strangers, but anyone who treats him as an ordinary human being will find him a most interesting and entertaining companion." The newspaper business gave him the opportunity to reach the public without having to make appearances.

W. R.'s support for the underdog reached new heights in his support of the Cuban revolution. Since the sixteenth century, Cuba had been a Spanish colony. The Cubans were now demanding representation in their government, which was under Spanish rule. In *Journal* editorials, W. R. called for American support of the rebels, reminding readers of the American Revolution with England. Tension between Spain and the Cuban rebels grew as Hearst's *Journal* began bolstering American support for Cuban independence.

Readership of the *Journal* suffered when the Spanish in Cuba jailed Sylvester Scovel, a reporter from the *World*. Hearst felt the competition even more when the

THE BIG TYPE WAR OF THE YELLOW KIDS.

This rendition of Hearst (right) and Pulitzer (left) as the Yellow Kids criticizes their influence on the Spanish-American War.

World created a "Free Scovel" campaign that attracted hundreds of readers. W. R. had to do something to counteract this publicity. He figured out how to sneak two *Journal* reporters into Cuba to find stories as stunning as Scovel's.

Hearst fantasized that the Cuban situation was his opportunity to beat Pulitzer once and for all. *Journal* reporters would dramatize the Cuban revolution more sensationally than *World* reporters did. They would write more exciting human-interest stories. *Journal* readers would find out all the details about Spanish murderers, rapists, and torturers before *World* readers did. The Chief showed his writers what he wanted by doing some writing himself, including a profile of a Spanish military leader that began: "Weyler the brute, the devastator of haciendas, and the outrager of women. Pitiless, cold, an exterminator of men." *Journal* accounts of the situation pitted the rebels against the Spanish government in a struggle of good versus evil.

His reporters followed the Chief's example of strong and colorful language. Although Spanish officials prohibited them from traveling beyond their hotel, reporters described scenes as though they were eyewitnesses. Of all the major newspapers, only the *Journal* and the *World* were willing to put up with Spanish restrictions— and to create stories when they could not uncover the facts.

Well-known artist Frederick Remington and a *Journal* reporter collaborated on a story about three young Cuban women who were allegedly stripped and searched by male Spanish officials as they sailed to the United States. The story and pictures hit Americans like a bomb. Talk against Spain rose to a fever pitch. A short time later, the *World* issued its own "bomb." They reported that the whole story about the young women was a ruse by the *Journal* to sell papers. They had interviewed the young women who were named in the *Journal* reports, and the young women denied that they had been stripped or searched by male officials. In fact, they had been taken to a private cabin and searched by women. Faced with the facts, both Remington and the reporter who wrote the original story for the *Journal* admitted that they had made it up. The Chief had no comment.

Discovery of the false report did not deter W. R. from his crusade against the Spanish. He continued to push for U.S. involvement in Cuba. In one issue of the paper, he quoted a senator saying that he supported American intervention in Cuba. The senator later replied: "It [the *Journal* article] is a lie from beginning to end." Hearst did not answer.

An often-repeated story is that Remington sent W. R. a telegram from Cuba saying that there was nothing to report so he wanted to come home. Supposedly, the Chief wired back, "Please remain. You furnish the pictures and I'll furnish the war." W. R.'s son, William Randolph Hearst, Jr., later said this story was untrue. No one ever found a copy of the telegram.

When W. R. discovered Evangelina, he believed he had a story that would ignite America to action. Evangelina was an eighteen-year-old Cuban woman

Frederick Remington provided drawings of the alleged search of three Cuban women by Spanish officials.

accused of treason by the Spanish. W. R. claimed that his reporters had found her in a filthy jail cell, half-starved, and in solitary confinement. The *Journal* encouraged American women all over the country to sign a petition demanding Evangelina's release. He sent a copy of the petition to the Spanish Queen Regent Maria Christina and to the American minister in Madrid, Spain. An editorial suggested that staff from the *Journal* might forcibly release the prisoner if necessary.

Women all over the country signed the petition. The *Journal* published twelve columns of signatures. Mass meetings were held, demanding that Evangelina be freed. The campaign exceeded even W.R.'s expectations, and his plan became an even grander victory for the *Journal* and for himself.

His aides bribed prison guards to let Evangelina escape and smuggled her onto a Hearst-owned ship. As soon as he heard that she was on her way to the United States, W. R. organized a massive celebration with bands, speakers, and thousands of supporters. *Journal* headlines shouted that the newspaper had accomplished in just a couple of weeks what the American diplomacy corps had not even dared to try.

His readers treated W. R. as an American hero. Demonstrators were as eager to hear from him as from Evangelina. But, the Chief could not overcome his shyness in a crowd. At the demonstration, he shook hands with Evangelina and left immediately.

Due to increasing public support for the Cuban rebels, on January 25, 1898, the U.S.S. *Maine* sailed into Ha-

Frederick Remington, whose drawings helped to sway public opinion about the Spanish-American War.

vana harbor on what the American government called a "friendly visit." Three weeks later, an explosion blew the *Maine* to pieces, killing 260 officers and wounding others. The first *Journal* headline, "Cruiser *Maine* Blown Up In Havana Harbor" was based on facts, but the next *Journal* headline stating that Spain was guilty of the bombing was not. (To this day, there is some doubt about whether the explosion was caused by sabotage or a mechanical problem on the ship.)

Even as the Spanish were denying any responsibility for the explosion, the *Journal* was calling on President McKinley to declare war on Spain. W. R. whipped up public frenzy against what he called Spanish treachery in the sinking of the *Maine*. He raged against the president and Congress for what he said was cowardice for not launching an all-out attack on Spain in Cuba. He paid five members of Congress to visit Cuba and to write articles describing the suffering of the rebels there.

Other newspapers were more wary—they wanted proof Spain was responsible. Edwin Godkin, editor of a competing paper the *Sun*, tried to reason with the public: "when one of [the yellow journals] offers a yacht voyage with free wine, rum and cigars, and a good bed it can get almost any one it pleases to go on the yacht voyage and serve on the committee. Every one who knows anything about 'yellow journals' knows that everything they do and say is intended to promote sales."

On April 11, McKinley yielded to public pressure, and he raised the question of war in Congress. On April 19, the Senate passed a war resolution by 42-35. The

Hearst offered a $50,000 reward to anyone who uncovered the cause of the explosion of the U.S.S. *Maine*.

House passed the same resolution by 310-6. The United States was at war with Spain.

W. R. was jubilant. He bragged that this was the *Journal's* war. He offered a $1,000 prize to the person who thought of the best idea for celebrating America's entry into the war. *Journal* circulation rose to a million papers a day.

Not stopping there, Hearst set a trap for the *World*. He printed a phony story about a military man named Colonel Reflipe W. Thenuz who was supposedly killed in a battle in Cuba. The *World* picked up the story from the *Journal* and printed it. Delighted, W. R. told readers that he had caught the *World* in the act of stealing news. To further humiliate Pulitzer, he explained that with a little imagination, anyone could read the alleged colonel's name as "We pilfer the news."

Intent on playing an important part in the war, W. R. wrote to President McKinley that he would pay the expenses to equip a cavalry regiment to serve in Cuba. He suggested himself as a leader, or at least a member, of that regiment. McKinley turned him down, saying that regiments would be chosen from all states equally.

W. R. concocted another plan. He offered the country his 138-foot-long steam yacht *Buccaneer* as a cavalry ship fully equipped and manned including guns, ammunition, and thirteen hundred horses. He suggested that he be named commander of the ship. The secretary of the navy accepted the offer of the yacht but reserved the right to choose his own commander.

W. R. would not stay in New York and watch the

"Hearst war" from a distance. He chartered the *Sylvia*, a large steamship, from a fruit company and set sail for the war zone with several reporters and photographers. On June 19, the *Sylvia* reached Kingston, Jamaica, and Hearst bought some polo ponies. The next day they reached Santiago, Cuba, where they interviewed two American officers. Hearst wrote an article praising the spirit of the U.S. sailors. He gave himself the byline "War Correspondent Hearst." He interviewed a commander of the rebels who praised the *Journal* reporters for their war efforts. Then Hearst rode to a battlefront, a notebook and pencil in his hands and a revolver in his holster.

He sent back dispatches that described him in the thick of the fighting: "here at our feet masses of American soldiers are pouring from the beach into the scorching valley, where smells of stagnant and fermented vegetation ground under the feet of thousands of fighting men rise in the swooning hot mists." The Chief was the only publisher sending back firsthand reports. He was establishing a reputation as an able and colorful reporter and as a courageous man who risked his life to get a good story.

W.R. scored another exclusive when, from onboard the *Sylvia*, he spotted a group of men on land, waving a white flag. Smelling a news story, he swam ashore, discovered they were Spaniards, and decided to take them to an American admiral. The Spaniards had meant to surrender anyway, and went peacefully. W. R. had a story. He left them on the American warship *St. Louis* and proudly accepted a receipt for twenty-nine Spanish prisoners. Then he sent his scoop to the *Examiner* offices.

When an article in the *World* reported that the 71st American regiment had not fought well in an important battle, the *Journal* immediately scolded the paper for criticizing the American military. Calling Pulitzer unpatriotic, W. R., who had not seen the regiment in question, praised it highly. Pulitzer then created a fund to raise a monument to the 71st regiment. Having the *World* right where he wanted it, Hearst published articles that made fun of Pulitzer's change of heart. Readership rose for both papers, but perhaps the *Journal* won the battle when it was able to report that the men of the 71st refused to accept the monument from the *World*.

According to the Chief's figures, circulation for the *Journal* rose to 125,000. The *World* claimed to match this circulation. But increased circulation did not guarantee profits since both papers spent heavily on war correspondents, transportation, dispatch boats, and extra editions—sometimes as many as forty editions in a single day. W. R. had no problem borrowing $7,500,000 from his mother. He assured her (and himself) that his reports on the war would boost advertising revenue to cover the expenses.

In a campaign to fund a memorial for the victims of the *Maine*, Hearst hired H. J. Pain, a noted expert in fireworks, to stage gala spectacles. A creation called *The Maine* featured twenty glowing battleships and booming gunfire. A *Journal* train took these shows all over the country, spreading the Hearst name far and wide.

By July, most of the Spanish troops in Cuba had surrendered, and American ships began to return home. Hearst asked his readers to take the day off to celebrate the return of the victorious fleet. He planned parades and demonstrations as the ships sailed up the Hudson River. The only way citizens could learn about the many activities of the day was to buy the *Journal*, which carried the schedule for the celebration. The crowds were enormous and Hearst was on top of New York City.

Chapter Four

Aspiring Politician

The end of the war brought more opportunities for Hearst. He campaigned about the poor conditions faced by the returning soldiers. Articles told of troop ships with bad water and supplies, and army reception centers with insufficient food and clothing. Hearst blamed some of the deaths of American soldiers and veterans on improper care by American military officials.

It seemed Hearst could use almost anything to sell papers. One of his editors, Willis Abbot, described how: "Your true yellow journalist can work himself into quite as fiery a fever of enthusiasm over a Christmas fund or a squalid murder, as over a war or a presidential campaign. He sees everything through magnifying glasses and can make a first-page sensation out of a story which a more sober paper would dismiss with a paragraph inside."

Abbot was right. The *Journal* quickly found new dramas: a woman convicted of murder and the question of her electrocution, the possibility of the United States taking the Philippines from Spain, and the precarious condition of the Brooklyn Bridge (on investigation it was found to be perfectly safe). Hearst also supervised the collection of funds for a national monument in memory of Americans who had died in the *Maine* explosion. He led a crusade to lower the fares of public transportation. He exposed the fraud of meat packers who were using city water without paying for it.

The *Journal* dramatized the expansion of New York City. In the late 1890s, Brooklyn, Staten Island, Queens, and the Bronx were independent cities. In 1897, they joined with New York City to form one huge entity 324 square miles in size with a population of almost four million people. The newspaper arranged for fireworks, bands, parades, and other celebrations. Thanks to the *Journal*, five hundred magnesium lights shone from City Hall, guns roared, skyrockets soared, and bands played in parades.

In 1899, W. R. told his mother he wanted to buy a newspaper in Chicago. She loaned him $20 million, realizing that this was probably a gift. After all, her son had not begun to pay back the eight million dollars she had "loaned" to him since his father's death. She confided to a close friend that she believed W. R.'s venture was madness. She worried constantly about the *Journal's* heavy monthly losses. She said that W. R. was losing about a million dollars a year and at that rate, she could help him out for about thirty years. Despite her reservations about his financial wisdom, she praised

Hearst dreamed of being William Jennings Bryan's vice-presidential running mate in 1900.

him for his exposure of fraud and his support of reform in his papers.

With the money for a paper in hand, W. R.'s dreams grew. Maybe 1900 would be the year he could begin to realize his political goals. A newspaper could be an integral part of his political machine. Democrat William Jennings Bryan was running for president again, and W. R. thought that he could jump in as a vice-presidential candidate. He liked the idea of a Bryan-Hearst ticket and he believed that Bryan needed him in order to win the election. Not all Democrats agreed, however. One major reason was that W. R. had no serious credentials for national office. Other reasons included his shyness, his inability to make good speeches, and his reputation as a less-than-reliable journalist. Besides, some said, how could a country elect a vice president who wore plaid suits and garish neckties? Democrats who supported him noted that the Chief had lots of money, lots of recognition, and the power of the press in his favor. And the word got around that his mother's mine in South Dakota seemed to produce a never-ending supply of gold. Those who knew her figured that she would be a heavy contributor to any campaign in which her son featured.

Phoebe also added to the reputation of the Hearst name as a benefactor. She gave money to a school for girls in Washington and founded kindergartens for both whites and blacks. In California, she donated money to architects and archaeologists, and she planned to build the largest girls' gymnasium in the country.

W. R. wanted a brand-new newspaper to portray a strong image, one that could take him from mayor to governor and, finally, to president. He rented a building, shipped presses from New York, ordered supplies, offered fifty-dollar-a-week salaries to journalists who were then earning thirty dollars a week, and created the *Chicago Evening American.*

He printed his name in large type on the masthead and gave himself a frequent byline. He had a ready-made audience in the National Association of Democratic Clubs, of which he was president, with their three million members. In his articles and editorials, he planned to emphasize his reputation as friend of the masses and enemy of fraud and corruption. He hoped this depiction would swing readers away from his weaknesses—shyness and inexperience in politics. He supported the party platform that opposed monopolies which cut out smaller businesses. He also accused Republicans of paying too much attention to international politics and not enough to national affairs.

On July 4, he distributed one of the first editions of his *Chicago American* at the Democratic convention in Kansas City. His hopes rose when Bryan was nominated unanimously, but fell when Adlai Stevenson of Illinois received the nomination for vice president.

Disappointed but still a strong supporter of the Democratic Party, W. R. worked for the nominated candidates. Despite the fact that he hated appearing on a podium, he gave speeches portraying Bryan and Stevenson as leaders who would bring prosperity to all citizens. He argued that Republicans William McKinley and his running mate, Theodore Roosevelt, were greedy businessmen who would ignore the masses. W. R. managed to overcome his shyness and help lead a rally for Democrats in Madison Square Garden. When he entered the hall, people stood on their seats to cheer. Amid fireworks and a gala display of lights and bands, W. R. and other Democrats addressed a huge rally, urging potential voters to elect Democrats.

When Bryan lost to McKinley, W. R. immediately started making plans to run in the next election. He reasoned that Bryan had lost the election because of his stance on the economy. William Randolph Hearst would not make such mistakes.

He was ready to run for election—but only after a vacation. Hearst indulged in shopping sprees across Europe and the United States. He spent lavishly to decorate his home, buying suits of armor, mummies, statues, vases—anything that took his fancy. And he took some time out to enjoy his favorite entertainments: vaudeville, comedy, theater, and light musicals.

When he got back to work, he encouraged his writers to criticize President McKinley. His papers claimed that McKinley favored big business over the middle and lower classes. Articles described farmers, factory workers, and laborers working in poor conditions for low wages and facing a continually rising cost of living. Editorials declared that these workers did not see a bit of the prosperity that McKinley said was sweeping the country.

In September 1901, President McKinley was shot to death by twenty-eight-year-old Leon Czolgosz. Some rumors blamed W. R. and his papers for creating anti-McKinley sentiments strong enough to incite a man to murder. In some cities, W. R. was hanged in effigy. His papers lost both circulation and advertising. Hearst thought the rumors would stop when Czolgosz testified, "I never saw a Hearst paper," but he was wrong. W. R.'s greatest worry was that this connection would be remembered when he was running for president. He was somewhat relieved when his newspaper sales returned to normal.

After Vice President Theodore Roosevelt was sworn in as president, the *Journal* continued to attack Republican policies, especially about the growth of monopolies. Hearst featured articles supporting labor unions and decent working conditions. His papers condemned big business when coal mine owners joined with railroad operators to coordinate the working conditions of miners and railroad workers alike. Hearst did not hesitate to give advice to the president. He urged Roosevelt to authorize a canal in Panama. At that time, ships traveling to and from California had to go all the way around the tip of South America. Hearst saw a transportation bonanza in a shortcut, a canal through Central America. In 1903, the United States signed an agreement with Panama to build the canal.

Hearst's question-and-answer columns focusing on women's problems were widely popular. He also continued to use shock and curiosity to sell his papers. He

In September 1901, President McKinley was assassinated by Leon Czolgosz in Buffalo, New York.

explained, "People are interested in the fundamentals, love, romance, adventure, tragedy, mystery. Whoever paints the world must paint the deep shadows as well as the bright lights." He once complained to his writers that a particular edition of the paper was so dull it was like reading a telephone book. The editors and writers involved in that issue immediately found, or created, more exciting stories. As photographs became more accessible, Hearst papers included more pictures. His Sunday supplements favored stories of the weird and bizarre—notorious criminals, physically deformed people, science fiction, cartoons, and comic strips.

At the same time W. R. was becoming more involved with the news and politics, he also fell in love. Although he was shy, forty-year-old W. R. asked Millicent Willson, a dancer in the popular *Merry Maidens* troupe, for a date. She agreed, but only if her sister Anita could go with them. The women were stunned when the Chief brought them to the *Journal* offices. Millicent described this first date: "He took us inside a dirty, noisy newspaper office, asked us to be seated, rolled up his sleeves, and began making all kinds of marks on sheets of print. This was no Prince Charming!" That first date didn't harm W. R.'s chances with the dark-haired beauty. A few weeks later, he proposed to her, and she accepted.

Like his father, W. R. had chosen a bride half his age. But the resemblance to his father's choice ended there. Millicent was a chorus girl with none of the polish and culture expected from a member of the Hearst family. A rumor exists that Phoebe sent her daughter-in-law-to-

Hearst married dancer Millicent Willson in 1903. The following year their first child, George, was born.

be to a finishing school for six months, hoping to make her more socially acceptable.

In April 1903, William Randolph Hearst married Millicent Willson in an Episcopal Church in New York. Millicent was a stunning bride, and W. R. a tall and handsome groom. The wedding was small with only thirty guests. Phoebe stayed home, pleading illness. After the ceremony, the couple sneaked away from the cameras and reporters, even those from the Hearst papers. They sailed to Europe for their honeymoon.

Even on his honeymoon, the Chief had his mind on business. In London, he became fascinated with a British magazine called *Car*. Immediately, he cabled his associate in New York to open a similar magazine in the States and to call it *Motor*.

Back in New York, he founded his sixth newspaper, the *Chicago Morning American*. He also became a candidate for Congress from New York's Eleventh District. This was a safe Democratic district with little need for campaigning, but W. R. was determined to make his name known in preparation for his run for the presidency. He campaigned widely, making as many as a dozen speeches a day. He stopped worrying about his voice that some had called girlish—his goal was to become known as a political leader. He switched from gaudy outfits to the more conventional attire of dull black broadcloth and a black hat. He succeeded in capturing three times more votes than his opponent.

With his eyes on the presidency, Hearst started his seventh newspaper, the *Los Angeles Examiner*. He sent one of his aides around the country to form William Randolph Hearst Clubs. In the *Examiner*, he continued to push for reform with an emphasis on helping the working man. He fought against the Consolidated Gas Company and the Ramapo Water Company, businesses that used illegal means to create monopolies. He defended overworked and underpaid workers in sweatshops. He urged the creation of more public schools. When police shot striking miners, he blamed the mine owners, saying that their working conditions made strikes inevitable.

In April 1904, the Hearst's first child, a son named George, was born. The baby was healthy and well loved. Hearst was proud of his son, and his letters to Phoebe were full of news about the boy. It almost seemed as if Hearst was finally settling down.

Chapter Five

Dreams of the Presidency

Once he assumed his seat in the U.S. House of Representatives, W. R. became a member of the Labor Committee. He followed his campaign promises to help working people by supporting an eight-hour workday. He also continued to support a graduated income tax, which meant the wealthy would pay more taxes, and he worked to more effectively represent the middle and lower classes. He also continued his strong opposition to monopolies—large companies that controlled entire industries. Hearst did more than attack monopolies with proposed legislation. He asked for a congressional investigation of the coal-railroad monopoly, and proposed government ownership of essential services like transportation, telegraphs, and water.

These ideas had been well accepted when he proposed them in his newspapers and on the campaign trail. So he was surprised when his fellow congressmen did not support him. There were many possible reasons for this lack of support. Some representatives still blamed him, at least in part, for McKinley's assassination. Some distrusted him because of his sensationalist newspapers. Others resented the fact that he only talked to them about business that mattered to him. Still others resented the idea that this freshman congressman was trying to tell them what to do, especially since he had a poor record of attendance at meetings.

The Chief was still preparing to run for president. In Boston, he created his eighth paper, the *American.* He asked his writers and editors to write more statesmanlike journalism which would create an image of himself as a presidential candidate. He traveled throughout the country, partly on newspaper business, partly on congressional business, and mostly to find delegates and other supporters for his potential candidacy.

In 1904, the California Democratic Party nominated him as their presidential candidate. If he could capture the national nomination as well, forty-one-year-old Hearst would run against President Theodore Roosevelt. Hearst could see his prize within reach. Although it would be close, he believed he could win the Democratic nomination if William Jennings Bryan supported him. Surely, Bryan would pay him back for all the support Hearst had given him. But Bryan did not. When nominations were called, he came out for Alton Brooks Parker, chief judge of a New York State court. Parker won the nomination.

W. R. did not even wait around the convention to see if he could secure the nomination for vice president. He traveled right back to New York where he tried to bury his disappointment in another project. Sensing that the downtown area would become increasingly valuable, he bought property at the south end of Central Park. This complicated deal could not keep his thoughts from politics and he began thinking about how to enter the 1908 campaign for president. He started by running for Congress again. He won easily, due at least in part to the enthusiastic support of his newspapers.

Immediately after returning to Congress, he introduced bills to support eight-hour work days, to imprison railroad officials convicted of fraud, and to allow the government to operate telegraph lines. Although his bills were defeated, W. R. received a lot of publicity from each one. He also gained supporters when his papers publicized letters proving that the wealthy Standard Oil Company had bribed a United States senator for his votes on bills that would favor the oil company.

W. R. decided to run for mayor of New York City. From that position, he would run for governor of the state. He knew that many of his Democratic colleagues would not support him, but the Chief had faith in his dreams. He believed that the masses—especially those who read his newspapers—would vote for him. He said, "The impossible is only a little more difficult than the possible."

In the spring of 1905, he bought his second magazine, *Cosmopolitan*. He also ran for mayor of New York City and was supported by Democrats who believed that his battles for reform had convinced his readers to vote for him. He campaigned for better schools, cheaper government, and lower utility bills. His opponents accused him of helping anti-government subversives and foreigners. Some called him immoral because of the sensationalist articles in his papers. Competing newspapers jumped at the chance to denounce Hearst. When Phoebe expressed concern for his safety, he told her: "Don't let us bother about the liars and blackguards. If a dog barked at me in the street, I would be foolish to get down on all fours and bark back." Nonetheless, he kept a gun on his desk within reach.

His opponent was Republican George McClellan, Jr., a former congressman and one-term mayor. W. R. rose to the challenge of the election. He trained his high-pitched voice to carry through large crowds, spoke intelligently, and showed new dignity and energy.

When the results were tallied, W. R. had lost to McClellan by fewer than 3500 votes. He declared that the election was corrupt and demanded a recount. The recount did not change the results. (Too late to help, a politician admitted that he had helped fellow politicians throw boxes of ballots into the river.) Although he had lost the election, W. R.'s political standing soared. He had made a fine showing against a strong political machine, and his campaign had shown political savvy and promise.

He kept his name in the public eye after a major earthquake and fire in San Francisco destroyed millions of dollars worth of property, including his *Examiner* building, on April 18, 1906. Using the facilities of a nearby publisher, Hearst missed publishing only one edition of the paper. He created fund drives to rebuild ruined structures, establish hospitals, and set up relief camps. He started *Farm and Home* to take the message of his generosity and public-spirited actions to the rural areas not generally served by his larger papers. His continued interest in the presidency was fortified by his concentration on moral issues. He ran stories attacking racetracks, nude figures in art, smoking, and drinking.

At the state Democratic convention in Buffalo, New York, W. R. was nominated to be the candidate for governor to run against Republican attorney Charles Evan Hughes. Those who supported W. R. broadcasted the issues he had been fighting for in previous campaigns: antitrust cases; keeping prices of railroads, coal, gas, and other utilities under government control; eight-hour workdays; and pensions for teachers. His opponents declared that he was an egotistical showman, intent only on pursuing his own ambition as a sensationalist journalist and politician. Despite this opposition, it looked as though Hearst might win.

Then Theodore Roosevelt sent his secretary of state to New York to speak for Hughes. This was the turning point. The Chief lost the election by 60,000 out of a total of a 1.5 million votes. Even Hearst heard the message from the voters. He declared he would never again run for office and criticized his opponents: "I congratulate the bosses on their foresight in defeating me, for my first act as governor would have been to lift

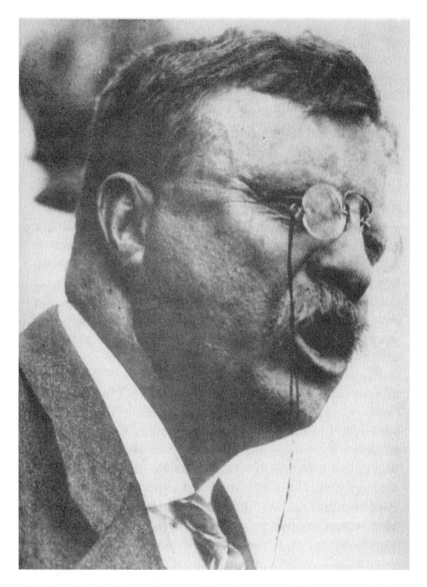

President Theodore Roosevelt supported Hearst's opponent Charles Evan Hughes in the 1906 race for governor of New York.

the dishonest officials by the hair of their unworthy heads."

In 1908, Hearst's second son, William Randolph Hearst, Jr., was born. W. R. wrote to his mother, "He has blue eyes and rather blond hair and a fair voice, a good appetite and a disposition to sleep his senses away." He rented more than thirty rooms on the top floors of an apartment house on Riverside Drive. There he could accomodate his growing family and household staff as well as display his art treasures.

Though he said he was done with politics, Hearst didn't give up his stand on reform. He became active in the Independence Party (IP) and merged it with the William Randolph Hearst League. He knew that neither group had a chance of winning a major election at this time, but he wanted to show some opposition to the Democratic and Republican parties. He hoped that the IP could steadily gain enough ground so that it could carry some influence in the 1912 elections.

In 1908, William Howard Taft won the Republican presidential nomination, and Bryan was once again the Democratic candidate. The Independence Party nominated businessman Thomas Hisgen of Massachusetts for president and John Graves of Georgia for vice president. Hisgen and W. R. campaigned together. At each stop, the newspaperman dominated, leaving Hisgen in his shadow.

In September, W. R. played his trump card. He publicly read letters that proved corruption on the part of Republicans in the matter of big business trusts. This revelation made headlines all over the country. Republicans were in deep trouble. Then W. R. disclosed letters that proved the Democrats were just as involved in the corruption as Republicans were.

Hearst kept up a steady stream of stories about corruption by the major parties and, as he had planned, the Independence Party gained supporters. W. R. was again in the national spotlight.

That spotlight, however, was not strong enough to sway the election, and Taft won over Bryan. Hisgen ran a very poor fourth, failing even to come close to the third-place candidate, Socialist Eugene Debs. Once again, W.R. was a loser. He realized, too late, that he had tried to do too much alone. He had tried to decrease the status of the two major parties and to increase the status of the Independence Party, without the kind of backroom bargaining necessary. He had abandoned the Democrats, shamed the Republicans, and failed in his attempt to promote the Independence Party.

Back in his offices, forty-five-year-old W.R. became more aloof. He encouraged fierce competition to get the most work out of each employee, and he was quick to fire any worker who displeased him. In addition, he adopted the habit of staring at anyone talking to him and showing no emotion at all.

Still, he did not give up his dream of becoming president, even though he had said that he would never again run for public office. At the back of his mind was a plan to exert power behind political scenes and thus to gain a reputation strong enough to cause others to encourage him to run. One of his ideas was to unite the Republican and the Independence parties against the Democratic Party. His old enemy Joseph Pulitzer tried to squelch his plans by printing articles in opposition to most of what Hearst said and did. True to character, William Randolph Hearst did not let the criticism deter him.

In 1909, despite his vow to never again run for public office, he ran a second time for mayor of New York City, and again lost. The defeat, however, did not affect his dream of becoming president. He believed that he still had time and the support needed to achieve the highest office in the land. Because he could not use the mayoralty as a stepping-stone to higher office, he would become a senator and move up from there. To create more publicity for his name and ideas, he bought the *Atlanta Georgian*, bringing the total of Hearst newspapers to nine.

In 1910, John Randolph Hearst was the third child born to W. R. and Millicent. Phoebe built a house for her grandsons on her estate in California with huge playrooms large enough to ride bicycles in. W. R. sometimes joined his family on visits to his mother, though his favorite place for relaxation was his San Simeon ranch with its grand view of the Pacific. He frequently entertained fifty to one hundred guests for a weekend there. They took a private train ride from San Francisco to the ranch and then limousine rides to their guesthouses on the property. Fishing, sailing, riding, tennis, swimming, and other pastimes were all available.

Hearst ran for mayor of New York City again in 1909.

Two years later, Hearst worked behind the scenes to oppose the nomination of New Jersey Governor Woodrow Wilson as the Democratic candidate for president of the United States. Hearst believed that Wilson, a former professor, was not shrewd or realistic enough to deal with the complicated European situation. W. R.

insisted that England and other potential United States allies were trying to drag America into a war. He opposed an alliance with these countries, declaring, "America First and Forever." In his latest publication, *Hearst's Magazine*, he wrote articles strongly condemning Wilson's international positions. To his despair, Wilson was elected.

Hearst immeresed himself in a new project to try to forget his political defeats. He decided that his thirty rented rooms at the Clarendon no longer were sufficient for him and his family. He bought the building and evicted the tenants on the eighth and ninth floors. He tore out walls to create a three-story room overlooking the Hudson that became a showcase for his tapestries, statues, paintings, and antiques. When he was an adult, William, Jr. described his experience in the house: "The top floors—Nine, Ten, Eleven and Twelve—belonged to Pop. But us kids, we had our own place. We had our apartments downstairs with Mom's folks. I suppose we were allowed up past the tenth floor around once a week. You know, Sundays and holidays."

Hearst expanded his business as well as his living quarters. As a contribution to the Panama-Pacific Exposition of 1915 in San Francisco, he installed a special color press on the fairgrounds. Spectators received hot-off-the-press copies of the latest edition of the *Examiner*. He also took advantage of a recent development in photography—motion pictures—to record events on the fairgrounds.

As conflict among European nations heated up, W. R.

opposed a growing popular belief that the Germans were preparing for all-out war. In his view, it was the British who were inciting the conflict. He found himself agreeing with his former opponent President Wilson. Both men believed that the United States should not become involved in a European conflict.

W. R. wrote articles describing Mexico as a potential enemy. He thought that the Mexican government might form an alliance with Japan against the United States. As economic problems grew in Mexico, W. R. capitalized on the unrest, warning that the Mexicans were preparing for war against the United States. He used his movie company, as well as his papers, to publicize his views. In 1915, his film company put out a film titled *Patria*, which described a Japanese-Mexican plot to overthrow the United States. Hearst was as involved in politics as ever.

Chapter Six

Farewell to Politics

In December 1915, twin boys Elbert Willson and Randolph Apperson were born to the Hearsts. W. R. wrote to his mother, "just at sunrise two of the loveliest boys you have ever seen were born to Mr. and Mrs. William Randolph Hearst." A few days later, he wrote, "I can't get used to the little things. They look so funny lying together on their little bed doing almost the same things at the same time in the same jerky little way, for all the world like miniature song-and-dance artists."

The twins did not slow down Hearst's ambitions. He continued to use the *Examiner* and his other papers to push his favorite issues. He encouraged the development of a national highway to meet the challenges of the fast-growing automotive industry. As usual, the Chief did more than write editorials to broadcast his position. He sent one of his cars, the *Pathfinder*, on a cross-country trip with many well-publicized stops where the driver encouraged support for a national highway.

Following *Pathfinder* visits, a number of states appropriated millions of dollars for highways. Nineteen governors supported the idea of a coast-to-coast road. Education was another important theme in Hearst papers. W. R. opposed a plan to close kindergartens. When he discovered that 15,000 children went to school hungry every year, he organized a campaign to encourage women's groups and churches to give children free lunches in school.

At the national conventions of 1916, W. R. had little influence. The Democrats renominated Wilson, hoping that he would keep them out of the war. The Republicans nominated Charles Evan Hughes, former governor of New York. The Hearst newspapers supported Wilson solely on the president's opposition to American involvement in the European conflict.

The papers continued to oppose what the editors viewed as British interference that pushed the U.S. toward entry into World War I. The British retaliated by closing their cable and mail systems to the staff of the Hearst papers. The French and Canadian governments did the same. The ban enraged the Chief. He ordered editorials in all his papers against shipments of American food and ammunition to Europe. With typical Hearst showmanship, he put on a great display of patriotism. He ordered that the mastheads be printed in red, white, and blue, and that the words of "The Star Spangled Banner" be printed at the top of each editorial page. He added small American flags on both sides of the date lines.

As American opinion tilted toward war, Hearst declared: "Our first duty is to maintain peace; our next duty is to prepare for war." On April 6, 1917, President Wilson asked Congress to declare war on Germany. After the United States entered the war, the Chief continued to criticize. He argued that the war wasted American lives and money. He said that it would only slow, not stop, the downfall of England. Still he urged loyalty to the American government: "We Americans will fight determinedly, desperately, heroically, as long as we honorably must, but our purpose in war should be peace—peace without aggression or aggrandizement—peace for our own people and for all mankind."

The Hearst family could not vacation in Europe because of the war, so they spent more time at San Simeon. When there, W. R. entertained with a constant round of riding, dancing, parties, and picnics. Sometimes he made movies using his guests for actors and actresses. Sometimes he worked on a model of the double-towered castle he planned to build at San Simeon. Perhaps he dreamed he would one day be king there.

Always on the lookout for glamor, he frequently went to the famous Follies of 1917. He enjoyed the humor of comedians Will Rogers and Eddie Cantor, the glorious sets, and the glamorous dancers. He especially liked beautiful Marion Davies, one of the dancers. He got to know her and became infatuated by her humor, her warmth, and her vitality. This infatuation created two problems. Of course, neither his wife nor his mother would approve if he had an affair with the actress. And

President Woodrow Wilson asked Congress to declare war on Germany and its allies on April 6, 1917.

if he ran for office again, as he was still determined to do, the public would not approve. Despite these concerns, he continued to court Marion.

Hearst bought the *Boston Advertiser* in 1917. The next year he bought the *Chicago Herald*. And the following year, he bought the *San Francisco Call*, the *Washington Times*, and the *Milwaukee Wisconsin News*. This brought his total to thirteen newspapers and six magazines. He also owned ranches, mines, and real estate. Although his managers took care of the business operations, Hearst always knew what was going on in each endeavor. He often ordered his managers to visit him—at any hour of the day or night—to answer questions and to give reports. He sent frequent advice to his employees that usually included warnings about being accurate, impartial, and clear, and commanding them to always be competitive. He said, "When you beat your rivals one day try harder to beat them the next, for success depends upon a complete victory."

In 1918, he announced that he was a candidate for governor of New York. Opposition flared loud and strong. His critics reminded potential voters that W. R. had shown both pro-German and anti-British sentiments—unpopular positions now that American was fighting with the British against the Germans. Once again, his effigy was burned in several cities. In Oregon, citizens set fire to piles of Hearst papers and magazines and danced around them singing "Keep the Home Fires Burning." Advertisers withdrew from his papers, creating a sudden shortfall in revenue. He was put under surveillance by the U.S. Attorney General. He discovered that a new butler in his home was actually a federal agent in disguise.

W. R.'s reaction was to proclaim that he loved to be investigated. He talked about how pro-American he was, reviewing his support of the draft and of United States military preparedness. He sponsored parades, luncheons, and dinners all over the country to display his patriotism.

At the convention in July, the Democratic nomination for governor went to Al Smith. Hearst had lost another election bid.

Phoebe made a deal with her son. For her part, she would cancel all his debts to her (she had loaned him more than $14 million since 1891) and pay off his other current debts of $2 million. For his part, he would never ask her for money again, and in three years he would give her $300,000 so she could build a new wing on the University of California Museum of Art and Anthropology. W. R. agreed.

World War I ended in November 1918. New York mayor John Hylan appointed W. R. chairman of a committee to welcome soldiers home. Citizens and officials were incensed that Hearst, the pro-German and antiwar man, had been given that honor. A group of citizens formed its own committee to greet the soldiers with Theodore Roosevelt as chairman. As criticism against him grew louder, Hearst grew louder in defense. One afternoon, W. R. went out into the harbor in a launch to greet the veterans. They returned his greetings warmly. Anti-Hearst forces scheduled a meeting at Madison Square Garden to protest against him. W. R. used his influence and money to fill the hall with returned soldiers who supported him. He hired hecklers to demonstrate against the protestors. To make sure that his read-

Hearst and his family were photographed in military uniforms during World War I in an attempt to prove he was patriotic.

ers knew his position, he editorialized, "We should have kept out of the war altogether, but that I could not accomplish, and I only got hated and berated for my pains. However, we do not mind that in the newspaper business. It is part of the game."

When President Wilson announced the Fourteen Points plan for peace, Hearst disagreed with it. His chief criticism was of the League of Nations, in which member states promised to come to the aid of any member that was threatened militarily or economically. As before the war, Hearst and his papers continued to advocate a clear separation of American and European governments.

In April 1919, seventy-six-year-old Phoebe died from pneumonia caused by influenza. The estate she inherited when George Hearst died had continued to grow. In her lifetime, she had given over $21 million to charities. At her death, she left over $11 million to her son. Once his mother had said, "Every time Willie feels badly, he goes out and buys something." W. R. did that now. He ordered an architect to build the castle he had long dreamed of at San Simeon. He hired workers to build quarries on the site to supply cement and crushed rock. Using large trucks pulled by four horses, the workers carted tons of building materials from steamer ships up the hillside. Hearst furnished lights for the workers, and for his own use later, with a sophisticated modern electric battery plant. He bought more art pieces and antiques, acquired more real estate in New York, and invested heavily in movies. To further Marion's career, he hired an expensive and well-known set maker, successful screenwriters, famous directors, and publicity people. He set her up in a studio apartment with acting tutors and coaches. He spent so lavishly that he found himself without enough ready cash to carry on his business. This time he couldn't ask his mother for money. He found another way out of the problem. He floated a bond issue, and people bought shares in his papers. From the sale of these bonds, he acquired $12 million in cash.

Hearst's interest in Hollywood was not purely personal. He had long seen that movies had the same kind of power newspapers did: they could tell people what to think. That kind of power appealed to Hearst immensely, and for some time he had been finding ways to seize and exercise it. One outlet he embraced was film propaganda.

When Wilson ordered America into World War I, he knew that the public would be reluctant to give up neutrality. He hired a former journalist, George Creel, to help convince the people of America that Germany was evil and the war was necessary. Creel became the head of the Committee on Public Information (CPI), and soon decided to open a film division to help spread his message. What made CPI scandalous was the close connection the men running it, especially in the film division, had to Hearst. Almost all of the top people had connections to Hearst because they had worked for his publications. The fact that Hearst newspapers, movie reels, and cameramen were getting the best shots and the exclusive footage only made the situation more suspicious. Soon it became clear that Hearst was the de facto leader of the CPI.

Once he had a taste of the power of film, Hearst was quickly obsessed with it. He began pouring money into the making of movies, particularly those that gave him the opportunity to propagate his political beliefs. The lessons he learned about propaganda from the CPI served him well, and soon Hearst films were notorious for their strong political content. When he was able to, Hearst even wrote some of the scripts. And, of course, Marion Davies starred in as many as she could.

He still had political aspirations. He sought the Democratic presidential nomination again in 1920. He received only one vote. James Cox, another editor, won the presidential nomination, and Assistant Secretary of the Navy Franklin Roosevelt won the vice-presidential nomination. Upon hearing the vote, Hearst began planning to win the presidency in 1924.

In the 1920s, the Chief hired each of his five sons to work on his papers. Bill, Jr. showed the most interest. When he was sixteen, he had told his father, "I'll tell you what my ambition is. It is to help you in your business, to be capable to do my part, and then some." Maybe his other sons also had ideas about playing significant roles in the Hearst enterprises. But their father was unable or unwilling to give them the opportunity to learn. He often had them moved from one department to another with no regard for their interests or abilities. He criticized them frequently, scoffed at

their achievements even as he gave them more respon-
sibilities, and complained that they were costing him
more than they were worth. Though they were unhappy
and dissatisfied, the sons felt they could not afford to
leave their father's business. He paid them more than
they could make anywhere else.

His sons were not his only family problem. In 1922,
W. R. thought seriously about divorcing Millicent so he
could marry Marion. For many years, his mother's cer-
tain disapproval had prevented him from making these
moves. Now Phoebe was gone, and W. R. told Millicent
he would like a divorce. She reminded him that they
had five sons together, and that she had invested many
years in his campaigns and business arrangements. The
answer was no. Then she asked to be driven to Tiffany's
jewelry store. She picked out the most expensive pearl
necklace in the city and said to the clerk, "I'll take the
string with me. Send the bill to my husband's office."

A short time later, Millicent and W. R. came to an
agreement that they would observe the formalities of
marriage although the union meant very little to either
of them. Although he would be away often, W. R. agreed
to be at the Clarendon enough to make it seem that the
boys had a "normal" home. Both he and Millicent would
attend each other's affairs—political meetings and fund-
raising events. She kept access to her husband's accounts and withdrew money as she wished. A corporation attorney sent her regular reports on the financial
situation of Hearst's businesses.

Satisfied with this settlement of his marriage and

family, W. R. turned his attention back to his newspapers. More than three million people in the United States bought a Hearst newspaper everyday. The Chief meant to make the most of this opportunity to influence citizens and government. He had long disapproved of drugs and had urged more effective restrictions on the sale of cocaine, morphine, and other narcotics. In 1922, his *American* published inside information about a drug ring, giving names of peddlers. These articles established Hearst's influence on the formation of America's antidrug laws.

As 1924 approached, Hearst renewed his political campaigning in earnest, hoping at least to become governor of New York, perhaps even senator, and, hopefully, president. He bought the *Syracuse Evening Telegram* and the *Rochester Evening Journal* to help build bases for his campaign. He made an offer to Governor Al Smith. He would support Smith for reelection if Smith would support him for Senator. Smith refused the offer without discussion.

W. R. found it difficult, if not impossible, to get along with the Democrats. He found Republicans troublesome, too. So again he put his faith in a third-party movement, the revived Independence League. He led the first meeting of that league with a delegation of five hundred citizens. In his speech, Hearst said, "The fundamental idea of the Independence League is independence—independence of boss rule, independence of corporation control."

Hearst bought a Texas paper, the *San Antonio Light*.

Poll watchers guessed correctly that this was part of his plan to run again for president. Hearst believed that Governor Smith might also want the presidency so he filled his papers with articles against Smith and with editorials telling how a Hearst presidency would change the country for the better. At the nominating convention, he sponsored a gala for six hundred delegates and their wives at the Ritz-Carlton Hotel. The delegates ignored both Hearst and Smith. They nominated John Davis of West Virginia for president and Nebraska governor Charles Bryan for vice president. Hearst left the convention saying that the two nominees were fine people, but they were too conservative.

His own political dreams did not interfere with his dreams for Marion's career. He planned the biggest extravaganza ever for the opening of *When Knighthood Was in Flower*, a silent film starring Marion. He renovated a theater by building a pit for a symphony orchestra and hanging some of his finest paintings in the lobby to create an intriguing art gallery. Two Hearst papers mentioned Marion's name seventy-three times in two days, always with praise for her performance and her beauty. Critics on other papers noted that, although she had the most expensive sets in the country, Marion never equaled the status of "America's sweetheart," Mary Pickford, another screen star. Hearst resolved to make Marion an even bigger star than Pickford.

As with politics, Hearst struggled with his competitive nature in his business life, too. His keen sense of rivalry left him continually pushing for higher circula-

Showgirl and movie actress Marion Davies began an affair with Hearst in 1917.

tion and more advertising for his papers and magazines. Politics within the offices were stressful as writers and editors struggled to outdo each other to impress the Chief. Sometimes he became violent, destroying chairs, or stomping around and screeching. Because he paid such high salaries, his editors and writers felt indebted to him and were afraid they might lose their jobs if they suggested changes. They never knew what to expect. One day he would tell them to create unforgettable stories. The next day he would tell them not to offend "nice people" by exaggerating.

When the *Daily News* beat the circulation of Hearst's *American*, the Chief opened a lottery to encourage new readers to buy his paper. The grand prize was $1,000. The next day the *News* announced its own lottery with a grand prize of $2,500. The *American* raised its prize to $5,000. The *News* raised its prize to $10,000. The *American* raised its prize to $25,000. Finally both publishers admitted that the lottery competition was too expensive. Each withdrew the lottery offers.

That lottery hurt Hearst's already shaky reputation. For several years, people had criticized him for being recklessly extravagant in his personal life while he claimed to understand the plight of the lower class that had to struggle to acquire the basic necessities of food, clothing, and shelter. They had criticized his openly inappropriate behavior with Marion Davies. Now they were appalled by the lottery. People talked about him, wondering what kind of person W. R. was.

Perhaps the answer, in some ways, was that he was

still a child. He had not outgrown his fantasies about having the grandest homes, the most successful businesses, and the most exciting romances. He never satisfied his desire to buy things—land, houses, art pieces, and antiques. He seemed to believe that he could always do as he wanted and always have what he desired. Some people suggested that he saw himself as a movie star and the rest of the world as a movie set.

These were the opinions of many of the people who knew him only as a public figure. Those who knew him as a newspaperman and frequent political candidate had these thoughts and others as well. Some noticed a change in his political leaning. They cited his change from supporting to opposing the graduated income tax. Was this because he would have to pay more taxes himself? They cited his new opposition to unions, specifically a union of journalists. Was this because he would have to accommodate his own workers more?

The criticisms mounted, but they did little to hamper his success. By 1923, Hearst owned twenty-two daily papers and fifteen Sunday papers in the United States. The combined circulation was about 3.5 million. He owned seven magazines in the United States and two in England. Among the biggest-selling magazines were *Cosmopolitan*, *Good Housekeeping*, *Hearst's International*, and *Harper's Bazaar*.

Although his profits were huge, he spent money almost as soon as he earned it. Hearst did little bookkeeping, preferring to believe that he would always have enough money for whatever he wanted. He kept buying real estate in New York and added newspapers nearly every year. He had two specially equipped yachts, one of them continually staffed so that he could take it out at any time, and a fifty-seven-foot motor cruiser. He bought smaller boats for his sons. He once bought a hundred shirts in one shopping spree. He spent millions on making movies, mostly because he loved to see spectacles, seemingly unaware that the general public was not ready to pay a premium price for admission to see them. When a financial adviser suggested that he stop buying art, he answered, "I'm afraid I'm like a dipsomaniac [alcholic] with a bottle. They [sellers of art] keep sending me these art catalogues and I can't resist them." He bought two giraffes, seven zebras, and five ostriches for his zoo at San Simeon. He donated a million dollars to the women's gymnasium at the University of California as a memorial to his mother. He also donated money to an Abraham Lincoln memorial in Illinois and to a Greek theater in California. Some believed that he made these gifts in order to keep his name prominent in these two politically important states.

He did not respond to widespread rumors that he had fathered a number of illegitimate children. Some of these stories claimed that Marion Davies was the mother, but they were never proved. Hearst continued to express admiration and respect for his wife and children. They carried on their lives without him most of the time. Like her husband, Millicent toured Europe frequently. She accepted invitations to visit several European leaders, including the dictator of Italy Benito

Mussolini, King Alfonso of Spain, and the Pope. By 1925, Hearst and Millicent were separated in all but legal terms. He lived in Hollywood year round and bought an estate on Long Island for his wife. Millicent spent Hearst's money lavishly, became prominent in New York society, and worked in many fund-raising campaigns for charity. The two exchanged frequent letters and phone calls and remained generally friendly, except when Hearst complained that she spent too much money.

It appeared that Hearst had given up on his political dreams. When a friend mentioned to him that he had run unsuccessfully several times, he admitted, "Yes. I'm afraid I was nutty three times." He did not even attempt to get a nomination in 1928. Al Smith, his old opponent, captured the Democratic presidential nomination. President Coolidge chose not to run. Hearst supported Republican nominee Herbert Hoover. In that election Hearst, at last, supported a winner.

Chapter Seven

World Events

Now in his sixties, Hearst became involved in international affairs again when the Mexican government seized properties along the U.S.-Mexican border. Hearst and others owned the land, but Mexican President Calles believed the land rightfully belonged to Mexican farmers. W. R. retaliated in 1925 by pursuing a campaign that was intended to expose fraud and corruption in the Mexican government. He wrote about alleged anti-American plots, including some, which he said, were instigated by Mexican President Calles with the collaboration of four American senators. He published alleged copies of documents from Mexican archives as proof. Congressional investigations showed that the Hearst articles had included material and sources that were neither valid nor reliable.

Hearst was called to Congress to testify. He declared that the documents he quoted seemed authentic. Congress persisted. Finally, Hearst's journalists admitted that all the documents they published were forgeries. Hearst neither attempted to explain further, nor did he apologize. The real story behind the Mexican documents has never been uncovered.

He lost even more public esteem by supporting lower taxes for the wealthy. Liberals who once had praised Hearst's crusades for reforms were especially incensed when rumors flew that W. R. had received tax refunds of over $600,000 for two years in a row.

It was time for a vacation. Hearst invited Marion and a group of her friends to go on a European tour. Among other attractions, he wanted to see St. Donat's castle in Wales, which he had bought for $120,000 sight unseen. Hearst happily explored the dungeons, stables, and art treasures of the castle.

In Paris, he uncovered and published a confidential French government memo describing a secret pact between Great Britain and France. The scoop turned sour, however, and outraged both the French and British governments from whom it had been stolen.

Back in America, he installed eighty telephone lines and forty radiophones at San Simeon. Now he could send and receive calls almost anywhere on the compound. He had pencils and paper placed all around so that he was ready to record his ideas and messages. He also had a teleprinter machine and short wave radios installed. With this equipment, he kept tabs on all his businesses, as well as his family.

Nonetheless, like so many other Americans, he was unprepared for a sharp downturn in the economy. In

October 1929, stock prices on Wall Street collapsed, and many stockholders were wiped out. This caused massive unemployment. The stock market crash eventually led to the Great Depression, the largest economic crisis the United States has ever seen. Hearst believed that this depression, however, was merely a short-term inconvenience. He had never worried about where his money was coming from, and he would not be easily worried now. He continued spending. He gave four hundred acres of land and $100,000 to Oglethorpe University (he had previously been awarded an honorary Doctorate of Laws by the university). He bought the Hotel Lombardy in New York. He commissioned his St. Donat's architect to install three tennis courts and a swimming pool, and to add dozens of bathrooms. He had 36,000 paving stones sent from Spain for his replica of a Spanish cloister, and he commissioned one dozen full-length oil portraits of Marion.

Eventually his expenditures caught up with him. He was in debt for $110 million. To get cash, he put together a deal like the one in 1924. He merged his newspapers under the name Hearst Consolidated Publications and issued bonds for the new corporation.

Hearst papers criticized President Hoover for failing to act decisively to avoid the depression. W. R. presented a plan to have the federal government appropriate $5 billion to create jobs for the unemployed. Hoover paid no attention to him or to his plan.

Perhaps to hide his disappointment at being ignored, Hearst took a group of friends to Europe again. He had

San Simeon, overlooking the Pacific Ocean, was Hearst's favorite home.

scarcely arrived in Paris when he was ordered to leave within four days. This was a rebuke for his publication of the secret British-French pact. He left with the firm intention of retaliating against the French. His expulsion from France gave him a lot of favorable publicity in America. He wrote about it in his editorial: "If being a competent journalist and a loyal American makes a man *persona non grata* in France, I think I can endure the situation without loss of sleep."

As he stepped off the boat in New York, demonstrators greeted him with praise for standing up to the British and French governments. The rush of publicity awoke Hearst's dreams of running for political office. He made speeches about how he and the Hearst papers had done America a great service by revealing the existence of the secret documents. As he traveled from New York to California, he stopped in several of the larger cities to give speeches and to celebrate his discovery and publication of the secret pact. Was he also campaigning for office?

"Hearst for President" buttons showed up all over the country. His supporters claimed that he was decidedly pro-American and politically independent. W. R. was encouraged, but cautious. He feared this support would be forgotten by the time of the national elections two years away.

Although bursting with political aspirations, he continued to keep tabs on all aspects of his newspaper business, constantly seeking a way to make more money. He asked his general manager of the *American* why there was no advertising in the comics section of the paper. The manager explained that few companies advertised merchandise for children. The Chief asked him to find out how many adults read the comics. A survey showed that eighty per cent of adults did. The papers began to sell advertising for those pages, and in a few years, advertising in the comics section brought in over $7 million a year.

In June 1931, he again took Marion Davies and a group of friends on a trip to Europe. They traveled to Germany, Italy, Holland, and England, this time avoiding France. He returned to America, sure that Europe was preparing for another war. He was angry because the Allies had not yet paid their World War I debts to America, and he believed they were already preparing to fight again. He was determined to prevent this war if he could.

Fortune magazine described W. R.'s wealth: "Mr. Hearst does not merely own newspapers. He owns magazines, radio stations, ranches, and New York City hotels. He owns mines and a warehouse full of antiques. He hires thirty-one thousand men and women for $57 million a year, and he has working for him nearly a hundred executives." Hearst worried about who would succeed him as head of this business empire. Could one— or several—of his sons do the job? George went to the University of California for just one year, Bill stayed for two years, John dropped out of Oglethorpe, Randy dropped out of Harvard, and Elbert dropped out of Yale. W. R. had done well without a college education. He questioned if it was necessary for his sons to have one. In light of these business worries, he reconsidered his political fantasies. He told one of his favorite editors, "I have no political ambitions. In fact if anybody tried to give me a political office, I would murder him and would consider the deed justifiable homicide."

But he did not remove himself from the political game. He believed that Democratic candidate Franklin Delano Roosevelt was too involved in the problems in Europe and too eager to go to war. Hearst supported Democrat John Nance Garner over Roosevelt for president at the Democratic nominating convention. He wrote, "I am for him because he is plain and direct and sincere and honest—morally and mentally honest." After a few convention votes during which no man received enough to win, Hearst did two things. First, he asked his managers if Roosevelt would promise not to interfere in Europe's affairs in return for Hearst's support. They said he would. Then he asked Garner to release his votes. Knowing that he faced defeat anyway, Garner agreed. W. R. threw his support to Roosevelt, who won the nomination. He won the election in November. Although he did not receive the nomination himself, Hearst was proud that he had played a part in selecting the president.

Shortly after Roosevelt's election, the president invited Hearst to visit him in the White House. Hearst looked forward to helping the new president make his plans for the future of the country. Hearst believed the only way to help the country out of the depression was

President Franklin Roosevelt (right) introduced the National Recovery Act to help ease suffering during the Great Depression.

to support businesses, which in turn, would supply jobs for the unemployed. The meeting, however, did not go as he hoped. "I was greatly disappointed," he reported afterwards. "The President didn't give me a chance to make suggestions. He did all the talking." W. R. had become a different man. In the past he had advocated positions, such as the graduated income tax, that favored the poor and the middle class over the wealthy. Now, in the 1930s, he was much more conservative. He began to fear that the U.S. was turning to socialism, which was peculiar because a younger Hearst had advocated that government take over vital industries, such as the railroads and the coal mines. These were the sort of actions that socialist governments took.

Without Hearst's advice, President Roosevelt introduced measures to help the poor. One was the National Recovery Act (NRA), which Hearst considered morally and politically wrong. Some NRA money went directly to employ people to work in government funded projects. Hearst wanted the money go to business leaders so they could create jobs. He complained that the Roosevelt administration "was doing this partly in the interests of relief and reform—and professedly altogether in those interests. But the fact is that shrewd and unscrupulous distribution of monies in politically made work is being employed to control the electorate." He said that farmers must have money for seed before they can plan the rest of their farms. Likewise, heads of companies must have money for machinery and buildings before they can consider hiring employees.

Taking advantage of the poor economy, the Communist Party in America registered its largest vote count ever in 1932. With typical Hearst exaggeration, W. R. predicted that America was entering a fatal struggle against Communism. He wrote: "the Communistic tendencies in our country may bring about a situation which would destroy our democracy—a democracy which has been the happiest in the world. Communism is a contagion like a disease." He claimed that he found evidences of communist infiltration (which he called treason) at the University of Wisconsin, the University of Illinois, New York University, and several others. He sent disguised reporters to colleges to try to trick professors into admitting they were communist sympathizers. He urged that all teachers take an oath of allegiance to America and that the government investigate any suspicion of unpatriotic attitudes.

Hearst was severely criticized for his crusade. Sometimes when a Hearst newsreel played in a theater, the audience hissed and booed. The American Federation of Teachers, the Newspaper Guild, the United Auto Workers, and other unions condemned him. Some of these organizations tried to spearhead a boycott against Hearst newspapers, even handing out "I don't read Hearst" stickers. Hearst paid no attention to his critics who said he was pushing the issue too hard, "whether anyone else makes the fight against Communism and mob rule or not, I am going to make it."

The Great Depression, and possibly the boycott, cut into Hearst's profits. His chief executives advised him to make immediate and significant cuts in expenses. Hearst could not, or would not, do this. In 1933, he was refused a loan of $600,000 even though he offered to put up San Simeon as security. He finally borrowed the money through the help of a friend. Further financial problems arose when his employees, members of the Newspaper Guild, asked for higher wages and more job security. Hearst remained adamant: "Frankly," he said, "I have always regarded our business as a profession and not as a trade union." About writing, he said, "I do not think it is such a trick to write. Anybody who can think can write. All you have to do is to have some thoughts which are worth putting into words." With no more communication with the guild, he left for Europe with a large party of family, friends, movie people, and nonunion newspaper colleagues.

While in Europe, Hearst received an invitation to visit Adolf Hitler, head of the Nazi party, who supported increased military and industrial power for Germany. The Chief did not want to become involved in European politics but he accepted the invitation, hoping to influence the party leader. At their meeting, Hitler asked why Americans disliked the Nazis. Hearst said it was because Americans supported democracy, not dictatorships. Hitler protested that he was not a dictator, but a democratically elected leader, who had to restrain citizens' freedom until he could establish a democracy.

In the articles he sent back, Hearst spread the word that Germany was not a country to be feared. Instead, he labeled France and Italy as threats. He reported that both these countries were building up a huge stockpile of arms. Public reaction ran strongly against the Chief for supporting Hitler. They continued to criticize him for opposing Roosevelt's plans for social and economic reforms. The conflict increased when critics showed pictures of Hearst living like a king and quoted his complaints against paying taxes. Hearst seemed to let the criticisms slide right off him. He answered simply, "What is the greatest hindrance to the return of prosperity? High taxation."

His taxes did not stop him from spending money. Working on his dream of making Marion the most beloved movie star in the United States, he invited influential movie producers to his estate on San Simeon, an estate he sometimes called "the bungalow." Hearst treated these producers like kings, hoping to convince them to give Marion the best roles available. This was not an easy goal. Some movie producers said that she was simply not a good actress. Others believed that her slight speech impediment stood in her way as talking movies became popular. Others noted that Marion did not have the kind of drive to succeed that Hearst did.

In this way, Marion and Hearst were different. She earned half a million dollars a year doing what she liked. Her schedule was easygoing: "Sometimes I would get to the set around eleven. Sometimes ten—sometimes noon. Then at luncheon we had banquets at the bungalow and we'd sit around talking about things. We wouldn't talk about pictures. We would get back on the set around three, do a scene or so, and then have tea about four-thirty." Hearst, on the other hand, worked very hard at his business and political endeavors, and took time to enjoy his wealth.

At San Simeon, W. R.'s zoo expanded to seventy animals, including tigers, yaks, and chimpanzees. His tennis court locker rooms provided tennis outfits for guests. The estate also included a kennel of purebred dogs, a private theater, an airstrip, thirty-five cars, and breathtaking gardens. A typical daily schedule on a party weekend started with the guests choosing their breakfast from a wide menu. Hearst and Marion appeared some time after noon, and everyone enjoyed a large buffet together. In the afternoon, they swam, played tennis, and simply relaxed. All the while, Hearst took part in the fun but was never far from a phone or teleprinter. After a late afternoon nap, guests enjoyed parties that usually lasted into the early morning. Often the theater held a special showing of a Marion Davies film. After everyone had retired, Hearst went into his study where he read newspapers and magazines and attended to memos and letters. Frequently, he would awaken an employee who had been in bed for hours.

Meanwhile, gossip grew about William Randolph Hearst and his personal life. There are conflicting stories about Hearst's possible fear of death. One rumor said that his friends and family knew that they were not to mention anyone's death in his presence. Some said that when an animal in his zoo died, he was depressed for days. There even a story that he hated to see trees die. Word went around that when a tree died, the gardeners at San Simeon painted the yellow leaves green until they could replace the tree.

It is true that Hearst loved animals. But maybe there was exaggeration in the anecdote that his staff spread table scraps around the grounds so mice could find food. Another account claims that every night a household worker put out special mousetraps that didn't harm the animals. Every morning these traps were transported about four miles away from the ranch, and the mice were released. Hearst's love of animals showed in his strong opposition to two popular pastimes: cock fighting and dog fighting. He dearly loved his favorite daschund, Helen. When she died, he told a friend, "I will not need a monument to remember her. But I am placing over her little grave a stone with the inscription—'Here lies dearest Helen—my devoted friend.'"

Chapter Eight

Legacy

Although he declared he would not run for office again, Hearst continued to try to influence politics and government. "I pointed out to the President," he reported, "that business was fearful of, and had no confidence in, many of his advisers and several members of his cabinet. I told him that business was being retarded because of fear engendered by [these men]." President Roosevelt answered that no one should fear or mistrust any members of his administration. But there seemed to be no way to bridge the gap between Roosevelt, who believed in directly empowering the lower and middle classes by creating employment opportunities, and Hearst, who believed in allowing the wealthy to create jobs and opportunities for the lower classes.

In the 1936 presidential election, Hearst supported Kansas governor Alf Landon, a Republican, against Roosevelt. Hearst believed: "Landon is genuine. Roosevelt is a fake." Hearst ordered his editors and writers to support Landon strongly. On the day before Election Day, Hearst predicted that Governor Landon would surely be elected president of the United States. The vote tally showed that F. D. R. got sixty-one per cent of the popular vote, and Landon, thirty-seven per cent.

Hearst was losing on another front, too. For several years, he had refused to recognize that his expenses often exceeded his income. His advisers may have tried to tell him. If they did, he did not listen. He had not shut down his newspapers that were failing. He had invested $50 million in New York real estate at a time when mortgage rates were high. He had spent another $50 million for art and antiques. After he was forced to study his financial situation, he tried again his ploy of issuing stock. The Securities and Exchange Commission refused his request. In 1937, seventy-four-year-old Hearst owed over $130 million.

Hearst had to hire a special financial adviser who immediately sold six of his daily newspapers. Then he sold eight more. He shut down Hearst's Universal News Service, and he stopped production on all his films. He made plans to sell off much of his treasure of art and antiques. Even the stones imported from the Spanish monastery were put on sale. He ordered Hearst to cut his living expenses by seventy per cent. W. R. refused at first, but then he agreed to try. Marion Davies sold off some of her holdings and presented Hearst with a certified check for $1 million. A welcome surprise, this check arrived just in time to prevent a foreclosure on some Hearst property. Then Marion sold some jewelry and created a trust fund that legally allowed her to give him another million dollars.

Hearst had just one public comment about his situation. He insisted, "The only thing I really seek now is to be a better newspaperman." He kept his remaining newspapers full of criticisms against high taxes, Roosevelt, Communism, and America's possible entry into the conflict in Europe. He wrote, "A fundamental policy of the Hearst papers is to keep America out of the war."

He started a column called "In the News" that became so popular he published it in some of his other papers as well. In this column, he wrote more personally than he had before. He wrote about his early days in newspapers: "The competition of journalism was a glad sport; and yet back of it all was a due sense of responsibility—a genuine desire to use the powers and opportunities of the press to serve and to save." He wrote about his role of publisher: "This supervising of a number of newspapers is very much like balancing a feather on the end of your nose. You cannot just put the feather there and expect it to stay." He told the public that the reason for selling his art treasures was that he was too old to manage them any more.

His art collections were not selling well in private markets, so a large portion of the collection was put up for public sale in London, at Gimbel's department store in New York, and in other United States cities. The sales took place between 1941 and 1945.

The Hearst Corporation controlled Hearst Consolidated, Hearst Enterprises, Hearst Publishing Company,

Hearst Metrotone News, and Hearst Magazines. Except for Hearst Consolidated, which owned about six newspapers, Hearst had one hundred shares of voting stock, a controlling factor, in each publication. He managed to hold on to this stock, seven of his residences, and twenty daily newspapers.

In these papers he kept hammering away at Roosevelt and the fear that the United States would be dragged into the European conflict. He believed Roosevelt's election to a third term in 1940 would be a disaster for the United States because he believed that Roosevelt would declare war as soon as he was reelected. He criticized the president as a man of vast ambition. He publicly asked Roosevelt not to run for a third term: "Mr. Roosevelt, for your own sake—for democracy's sake—for America's sake—begin the battle against dictatorship here at home."

In the 1940 election, Hearst thought he was ready to support anybody but Roosevelt. Then he met Roosevelt's opponent, Republican Wendell Willkie. He wrote: "So Mr. Willkie has a pleasant smile and parts his hair neatly, but people are not going to vote for him because of the way he parts his hair and smiles, but because of what is behind the smile." Roosevelt won over Willkie by 27 million to 22 million votes.

On December 7, 1941, the Japanese attacked American sailors at Pearl Harbor. Hearst announced in his column: "Well, fellow Americans, we are in the war and we have to win it."

The war that Hearst had opposed brought him from

financial despair to soaring profits. High employment because of military production gave Americans spending money, and Hearst found more and bigger advertisers. Circulation rose. Before long, the Chief once again had money to spend. He built a wing onto his mansion at Casa Grande to display the art treasures he would buy to replace those he had recently sold. He also spent money generously on gifts, especially to educational institutions and hospitals.

In 1941, the Orson Welles movie *Citizen Kane* portrayed the life of a man much like Hearst. The hero was a wealthy newspaper publisher who craved political power. This character, who left his wife to marry a young singer, was arrogant, hot-tempered, and without moral convictions. People asked over and over: Was Citizen Kane really William Randolph Hearst?

Just when his finances were no longer a problem, Hearst discovered a serious personal problem. Doctors found an irregular heartbeat that they could not change. They gave him orders to rest, watch his diet, stay free from stress, and exercise (but just a little). Hearst did not take orders easily, even from his doctors. Marion had also developed a drinking problem that added to his stress. As hard as he tried, Hearst was not able to help her.

Maybe it was partly because of Marion's problems, but his advisers were finally able to convince Hearst to make a will. He had always refused before, saying there was no reason to do so. Now his advisers gave him two reasons. One was Marion, and the other was that taxes would take about $50 million from his estate if he died without one. Hearst relented and spent three years with several trusted advisers working up a 125-page document, the longest will ever filed in California. He left his wife $7.5 million and some Hearst Corporation shares. To his sons he left about $30,000 a year each in income guaranteed by a trust. He left voting shares of the Hearst Corporation in a trust controlled by a board of his sons and six Hearst executives. He also left large amounts of money in trust to educational and charitable institutions, including the University of California and the Los Angeles Museum. In that will, he left nothing to Marion; he had earlier provided for her with a trust fund giving her a lifetime income from shares of Hearst stocks.

In 1947, Hearst moved into Marion's Beverly Hills home. Despite her drinking, the couple remained devoted to each other. She signed a photograph for him "my love [for you] is deep; the more I give to thee, the more I have, for both are infinite." He often slipped love notes under her bedroom door.

As the years passed, Hearst had less energy. His secretary kept letters and memos traveling around the country so that he was in touch with all his offices whenever he felt able to communicate. He telephoned members of his staff at any hour of the day or night, whenever an idea struck him and he felt strong enough for a conversation. As much as he could, Hearst supervised sixteen large daily newspapers, three radio stations, and eight magazines.

His grandson Bunky, Randolph's son, asked him for a job on one of his newspapers. Hearst eagerly accepted his enthusiasm. He had advice too: "If you want to be a newspaperman, don't go to journalism school. Learn all you can while you are working. In five months you can pick up everything they can teach you in a school. Watch everything, ask questions, and learn why. That is the way I did it, and I think it's the best way."

Even when he needed a wheelchair, Hearst kept contact with his businesses. After four years' illness, he weighed only one hundred twenty-five pounds and he seldom left his bed. He dictated letters and orders even as his voice became weaker and weaker. He said "I am getting old, running down, going to sleep like a top before it keels over."

William Randolph Hearst died in August 1951 at the age of eighty-eight. The cause of death was listed as brain hemorrhage. His body lay in state at the Grace Episcopal Cathedral on Nob Hill in San Francisco where hundreds passed by to pay their respects. As the services began, Hearst businesses all over the country observed a moment of silence. He was buried beside his parents in the huge marble Hearst mausoleum south of the city.

An obituary in the *San Francisco Chronicle* wrote that Hearst "came into American journalism with both fists swinging, that American journalism will never be the same as it was before it felt his hurtling impact, and that the era has been a more colorful, more zestful time to live in for his having been part of it."

In his later years, Hearst ran his publishing empire from his beloved San Simeon.

For many years, William Randolph Hearst lived in between reality and dreams. He dreamed of becoming the president of the United States, the most widely read publisher in the world, creator of the most spectacular movies ever seen, and protector of the public against fraud and corruption. He achieved many of his dreams during his lifetime: he was a frequent candidate for mayor, governor, senator, and president, affording himself a wide platform from which to make his views known. He managed forty-one newspapers and magazines read by twenty-one million people. He was active in the production of movies. He was the creator of many reform movements that benefited middle and lower class citizens, and a proponent of capitalist enterprise.

As he grew older, he grew more realistic. After years of unsuccessfully campaigning for public office, he declared, "I will never again be a candidate." After pages and pages of editorials supporting reforms, he told his staff: "We have had too many crusades, especially critical crusades." Hearst went from attracting readers by sensationalism to praising the simple truth: "Truth," he said, "is not only stranger than fiction, it is much more interesting."

The legacy of Hearst's kind of newsmaking is still seen in our media today. While most of our mainstream newspapers pride themselves on reporting only the facts, as objectively as possible, they still have to determine what the facts are (which is often difficult) and to decide which stories to cover, a decision which is often political. Hearst made no attempt to conceal his poitical bias and used his newspapers to advocate his point of view on political and social issues, as well as to promote his own ambitions and wealth. The tabloid journals, television news magazines, and talk radio of today are the direct descendants of the Hearst and Pulitzer newspapers.

William Randolph Hearst made a lasting impact on journalism as well as on the American people. His efforts to give voice to the often ignored and powerless encouraged reform and the wider expansion of rights and prosperity. However, his manipulation of the news and distortion of facts sowed the seeds of a more troubling and dangerous legacy: how citizens are informed about the critical events and issues of their time.

Sources

CHAPTER ONE: Willie

p. 10, "Bless his little heart..." W. A. Swanberg, *Citizen Hearst* (New York: Charles Scribner's Sons, 1961), 7.

p. 10, "I scarcely ever leave Willie..." Judith Robinson, *The Hearsts: An American Dynasty* (Delaware: University of Delaware Press, 1991), 96.

p. 12, "If b-u-r-d doesn't spell ..." Swanberg, *Citizen Hearst,* 3.

p. 12, "We will study all the time..." Ibid., 14.

p. 14, "he wanted to give..." Edmond D. Coblentz, *William Randolph Hearst: A Portrait in His Own Words* (New York: Simon and Schuster, 1952), 9.

p. 14, "I'd like to put out..." Cora M. Older, *William Randolph Hearst: American* (New York: Books for Libraries Press, 1936), 34.

p. 16, "Bunny [Willie's rabbit] took some..." Robinson, *The Hearsts,* 158.

p. 20, "I am beginning to get..." Swanberg, *Citizen Hearst,* 24.

p. 20, "My financial condition is the same..." Ibid., 27.

p. 20, "I think I shall take..." Robinson, *The Hearsts,* 183.

p. 21, "your reformed child..." Ibid.

p. 21, "Show this to Papa..." Older, *William Randolph Hearst,* 50.

p. 21, "Will you kindly take..." Robinson, *The Hearsts,* 194.

p. 21, "Now there are two of..." Swanberg, *Citizen Hearst,* 28.

p. 23, "If you should make..." Coblentz, *William Randolph Hearst,* 28.

p. 23, "Well, good-by..." Ibid., 30.

p. 23, "I want the San Francisco..." Swanberg, *Citizen Hearst,* 33.

p. 24, "It's a wonderful mine..." Older, *William Randolph Hearst,* 67.

CHAPTER TWO: Newspaperman

p. 25, "One year from the day..." Ibid., 67.

p. 25, "The Largest, Brightest and Best..." Lindsay Chaney and Michael Cieply, *The Hearsts: Family and Empire–The Later Years* (New York: Simon and Schuster, 1981), 32.

p. 26, "this young Harvard man..." Older, *William Randolph Hearst,* vii.

p. 26, "We don't want fine writing.." Swanberg, *Citizen Hearst,* 59.

p. 28, "I had to get the people..." Robinson, *The Hearsts,* 213.

p. 28, "the most elaborate local..." Swanberg, *Citizen Hearst,* 42.

p. 28, "I don't suppose..." Older, *William Randolph Hearst,* 79.

p. 28, "The newspaper business is..." Robinson, *The Hearsts,* 210.

p. 28, "I will constitute a revolution..." Older, *William Randolph Hearst,* 79.

p. 31, "He is going too far..." Swanberg, *Citizen Hearst,* 68.

p. 32, "The *Examiner* was a madhouse..." Ibid., 71.

p. 32, "I am probably one..." Coblentz, *William Randolph Hearst,* 2.

CHAPTER THREE: Newspaper War

p. 35, "bankrupt his mother..." Older, *William Randolph Hearst,* 139.

p. 38, "He [Hearst] can't last..." Ibid., 144.

p. 38, "You cannot take a woman's son..." Ibid., 335.

p. 39, "He is genuinely shy..." Swanberg, *Citizen Hearst,* 378.

p. 41, "Weyler, the brute..." Ibid., 10.

p. 42, "It [the *Journal* article] is a lie..." Ibid., 114.

p. 42, "Please remain..." Robinson, *The Hearsts,* 324.

p. 46, "when one of [the yellow journals]..." Swanberg, *Citizen Hearst,* 141.

p. 49, "here at our feet..." Robinson, *The Hearsts,* 327.

CHAPTER FOUR: Aspiring Politician

p. 52, "Your true yellow journalist..." Swanberg, *Citizen Hearst,* 161.

p. 58, "I never saw a Hearst paper." William Randolph Hearst, Jr. with Jack Casserly, *The Hearsts: Father and Son* (Boulder, Colorado, Roberts Rinehart Publishers, 1991), 46.

p. 60, "People are interested..." Swanberg, *Citizen Hearst,* 195.

p. 60, "He took us inside..." Hearst, Jr., *The Hearsts,* 235.

CHAPTER FIVE: Dreams of the Presidency

p. 66, "The impossible is only..." Older, *William Randolph Hearst,* 129.

p. 67, "Don't let us bother..." Ibid., 302.

p. 68-69, "I congratulate the..." Hearst, Jr., *The Hearsts,* 49.

p. 70, "He has blue eyes..." Coblentz, *William Randolph Hearst,* 69.

p. 74, "America First and Forever." Hearst, Jr., *The Hearsts,* 51.

p. 74, "The top floors..." Chaney, *The Hearsts,* 60.

CHAPTER SIX: Farewell to Politics

p. 76, "just at sunrise..." Coblentz, *William Randolph Hearst,* 76.

p. 76, "I can't get used..." Ibid.

p. 78, "Our first duty..." Older, *William Randolph Hearst,* 374.

p. 78, "We Americans will fight..." Coblentz, *William Randolph Hearst,* 89.

p. 80, "When you beat your rivals..." Older, *William Randolph Hearst,* 358.

p. 83, "We should have kept out..." Coblentz, *William Randolph Hearst,* 90-91.

p. 83, "Every time Willie feels badly..." Swanberg, *Citizen Hearst,* 382.

p. 85, "I'll tell you what..." Chaney, *The Hearsts,* 64.

p. 86, "I'll take the string..." Ibid., 57.

p. 87, "The fundamental idea..." Older, *William Randolph Hearst,* 287.

p. 90, "nice people" Swanberg, *Citizen Hearst,* 355.

p. 92, "I'm afraid I'm like..." Ibid., 365.

p. 93, "Yes, I'm afraid I was..." Coblentz, *William Randolph Hearst,* 41.

CHAPTER SEVEN: World Events

p. 98, "If being a competent journalist..." Coblentz, *William Randolph Hearst,* 98.

p. 99, "Mr. Hearst does not merely..." Chaney, *The Hearsts,* 39.

p. 100, "I have no political ambitions..." Coblentz, *William Randolph Hearst,*123.

p. 100, "I am for him because..." Ibid., 122.

p. 102, "I was greatly disappointed..." Ibid., 154.

p. 102, "was doing this partly..." Ibid., 170.

p. 103, "the Communistic tendencies..." Ibid., 114.

p. 103, "whether anyone else..." Swanberg, *Citizen Hearst,* 477.

p. 104, "Frankly, I have always regarded..." Ibid., 442.

p. 104, "I do not think it is such a trick..." Ibid., 473.

p. 105, "What is the greatest..." Coblentz, *William Randolph Hearst,* 247.

p. 105-106, "Sometimes I would get..." Chaney, *The Hearsts,* 83.

p. 107, "I will not need a monument..." Coblentz, *William Randolph Hearst,* 244.

CHAPTER EIGHT: Legacy

p. 108, "I pointed out to the President..." Coblentz, *William Randolph Hearst,* 176.

p. 108, "Landon is genuine." Ibid., 184.

p. 110, "The only thing I really..." Hearst, Jr., *The Hearsts,* 59.

p. 110, "A fundamental policy..." Coblentz, *William Randolph Hearst,* 273.

p. 110, "The competition of journalism..." Swanberg, *Citizen Hearst,* 496.

p. 110, "This supervising of a number..." Coblentz, *William Randolph Hearst,* 267.

p. 111, "Mr. Roosevelt, for your own..." Ibid., 222.

p. 111, "So Mr. Willkie has a pleasant..." Ibid., 224.

p. 111, "Well, fellow Americans..." Swanberg, *Citizen Hearst,* 499.

p. 113, "my love [for you]..." Ibid., 517.

p. 114, "If you want to be..." Chaney, *The Hearsts,* 276.

p. 114, "I am getting old..." Older, *William Randolph Hearst,* 560.

p. 114, "came into American..." Hearst, Jr., *The Hearsts,* 253.

p. 116, "I will never again..." Swanberg, *Citizen Hearst,* 253.

p. 116, "We have had too many..." Coblentz, *William Randolph Hearst,* 261.

p. 116, "Truth is not only stranger..." Ibid., 268.

Bibliography

Chaney, Lindsay and Cieply, Michael. *The Hearsts: Family and Empire—The Later Years.* New York: Simon and Schuster, 1981.

Coblentz, Edmond D., ed. *William Randolph Hearst: A Portrait in His Own Words.* New York: Simon and Schuster, 1952.

Davies, Marion. *The Times We Had: Life with William Randolph Hearst.* New York: The Bobbs-Merrill Company, Inc., 1975.

Hearst, William Randolph, Jr. with Jack Casserly. *The Hearsts: Father and Son.* Boulder, Colorado: Roberts Rinehart Publishers, 1991.

Newseum. *Extra! Extra!* Virginia: Freedom Forum, 1997.

Nasaw, David. *The Chief: The Life of William Randolph Hearst.* New York: Houghton Mifflin Company, 2000.

Older, Mrs. Fremont. *William Randolph Hearst: American.* Freeport, New York: Books for Libraries Press, 1936.

Robinson, Judith. *The Hearsts: An American Dynasty.* Newark, Delaware: University of Delaware Press, 1991.

Schudson, Michael. *Discovering the News: A Social History of American Newspapers.* New York: Basic Books, Inc., Publishers, 1967.

Swanberg, W.A. *Citizen Hearst.* New York: Charles Scribner's Sons, 1961.

Whitelaw, Nancy. *Joseph Pulitzer and the* New York World. Greensboro: Morgan Reynolds, Inc., 1999.

Whitelaw, Nancy. *Let's Go! Let's Publish!: Katharine Graham and the* Washington Post. Greensboro: Morgan Reynolds, Inc., 1999.

Index